CW00543795

The Seasonal Festivals in Early Childhood:
Seeking the Universally Human

edited by Nancy Foster

Editor: Nancy Foster
Managing Editor: Lory Widmer
Graphic Design: Sheila Harrington
WECAN Administrative Support: Melissa Lyons

© 2010 Waldorf Early Childhood Association of North America
First English Edition

We gratefully acknowledge the authors and translators who allowed us to include their work,
and the publishers who granted permission to use the following:

Acorn Hill Waldorf Nursery and Kindergarten: "Hark children, sweet music" from *Let Us Form a Ring* (1989).

Freies Geistesleben: "Advent" and "Spring Awakening" by Freya Jaffke,
translated from *Feste im Kindergarten und Elternhaus, Teil 1* (1993).

Floris Books: excerpt from *The Christian Year* by Evelyn Capel (1967).

Wynstones Press: "At the Manger," words from "Softly, softly, through the darkness"
and "From Heaven's Arch So High" from *Winter*, third ed., 1999.
"Rain Flow" from *Spring*, third ed., 1999.
"The Heavens Above and the Earth Below," from *Summer*, second ed., 1983.
"Flaming Light" from *Summer*, third ed., 1999.

Published in the United States by the Waldorf Early Childhood Association of North America
285 Hungry Hollow Road, Spring Valley, NY 10977
This publication is made possible through a grant from the Waldorf Curriculum Fund.

ISBN 978-0-9796232-9-5

10 9 8 7 6 5 4 3 2 1

Table of Contents

The Seasonal Festivals in Early Childhood: An Introduction
Nancy Foster..v

The Cycle of the Year

Festivals for Young Children and the Cycle of the Year
Marjorie Thatcher...3

Festivals of the Year
Joan Almon...5

The Rhythm of Life
Helle Heckmann...9

Festivals
Stephen Spitalny...11

Working with the Cycle of the Year in Southwest Florida
Anne Savage...15

Celebrating Festivals with Young Children: Notes from a Conference
Nancy Foster...21

Finding the Realm of the Spirit of Humanity
from lectures by Michaela Glöckler...25

Autumn: Harvest time and Michaelmas

Celebrating the Harvest
Freya Jaffke...31

The Harvest Observance
Helle Heckmann...35

St. Michael on the Crescent of the Moon
from a Polish Legend..39

Images of Michaelmas
Nancy Foster...41

Taming the Dragon: Michaelmas in the Kindergarten
Barbara Klocek..43

Michaelmas Circle
Barbara Klocek...45

Michael and the Dragon
adapted from a Polish tale by Nancy Foster................................49

Michaelmas in the Nursery: A Celebration of Courage
Carol Grieder-Brandenberger..51

Michaelmas Story
Bella Schauman...55

A Michaelmas Festival for the Parent/Child Group
Cecelia Karpoff and Nancy Foster..57

George and the Apples: A Michaelmas Story for Puppets
Cecelia Karpoff..59

Winter: Advent, Christmas, and Three Kings Day

Advent: Preparation for the Adult
Freya Jaffke...65

The Turning of the Year: Midwinter and New Birth
Nancy Foster..69

Thoughts about an Advent Festival
Stephen Spitalny..71

Choosing a New Name for the Advent Garden
Nancy Foster..75

Stars for the Advent Garden
Susan Silverio..77

The Advent Garden and the Lyre: Something of the History
Christof-Andreas Lindenberg...79

Music for the Advent Garden
Edmund Pracht and Karl Schubert..83

Building Community through the Advent Garden
Joyce Gallardo..85

A Story for the Evergreen Garden
Joan Almon..89

Poems for the Midwinter Garden
Nancy Foster and Cecelia Karpoff 91

Creating a World Family at Advent Time
Holly Koteen-Soulé 93

The Little Sun Child
Sue Conroy Moran and Cathy Bower 95

Advent Circle for a Parent/Child Class
Nancy Foster 99

Advent Table Play
Nancy Foster 103

Changing Aspects of the Winter Season
Nancy Foster 107

The Legend of Babouschka
adapted by Ruth Ker 109

Three Kings Puppet Play for a Parent/Child Group
Cecelia Karpoff 113

Spring/Summer: Easter and Whitsun

Spring Awakening
Freya Jaffke 119

Seeking the Essence of the Festivals: Easter and Whitsun in the Kindergarten
Barbara Klocek 125

Searching for the Secret of Rebirth and Renewal
Holly Koteen-Soulé 129

Lady Spring Visits the Kindergarten
Marjorie Thatcher 133

A Story of the Easter Hare 135

The Easter Rabbit 137

Bringing Easter into the Nursery: A Universal Celebration of Spring
Carol Grieder-Brandenberger 141

Celebrating Spring in the Parent/Child Class
Nancy Foster 145

Celebrating the Whitsun Festival
Marjorie Thatcher 147

King Adder 149

A Summer Festival in the Parent/Child Class
Nancy Foster 151

Summer Circle for a Parent/Child Class
Nancy Foster 155

References and Recommended Resources 161

The Seasonal Festivals in Early Childhood: An Introduction

O ne of the wonderful, and wonderfully challenging, characteristics of Waldorf early childhood education is that there is no curriculum; we have no specific outline of activities or subjects offered by Rudolf Steiner for these early years. Rather, it is sometimes said that "the curriculum is the teacher." To that I might add two other elements, forming a threefold curriculum: the teacher, the developing child, and the social and cultural community, including the parents, surrounding the school or program.

The teacher, striving inwardly and outwardly to be worthy of imitation, creates an environment in which each child may feel recognized and held in a mood of dream-consciousness. The child, developing according to lawful, archetypal stages, yet a unique individuality, leads the deeply-observant teacher to provide nourishing surroundings and activities. And the school community, offering its particular mix of culture, race, religion, ideals, and questions, all within a specific geographic location, provides a social context within which the teacher and children are active together.

In the earlier years of Waldorf early childhood education in North America we looked to our European mentors and colleagues for guidance and inspiration out of their deeply-grounded experience. Many of us took up their offerings with gratitude and great joy. For me, as a beginning teacher, the whole concept of "festivals" was new, and I was awed by the richness of what I assumed were Waldorf traditions for celebrating these special times of the year. Especially abundant were the possibilities for observing Advent and Christmas.

Only later did we come to realize that many of these beautiful festival observances did not originate in Waldorf education but were European cultural and religious traditions. The European Waldorf schools were embedded in what was then a relatively homogeneous society, and it was natural that the traditions of that time and place found their way into the schools, where the teachers experienced them deeply, enriched them through their work with Rudolf Steiner's insights, and brought them to the children in a living way.

Today in North America we live in a diverse society, in widely disparate geographical areas with correspondingly distinct climates, each school surrounded by its own configuration of natural and cultural conditions.

The inner and outer work of teachers continues to be guided by our commitment to anthroposophy and Waldorf pedagogy. The growth and development of the children in our care still follow the archetypal laws revealed to us by Rudolf Steiner's research. At the same time, the realities of our school communities present us with a context that challenges and inspires us to re-examine some of our cherished festival traditions in order to welcome and include fully every child and family.

For many Waldorf early childhood teachers, this is a matter for research, a challenge to look ever more deeply into our own festival life as adults and how we bring this into our work with the children and families of our schools. We seek a growing understanding not only of the meaning and significance of the cardinal points of the year and their seasonal festivals— Michaelmas/Harvest, Advent/Christmas, Easter/Spring, and Whitsun/St. John's/Midsummer—but also of the nature and task of early childhood.

Our question becomes: How can we penetrate to an experience of these seasonal festivals that will be meaningful and nourishing for families of every background, and how can we bring this experience into the life of the young child in a developmentally appropriate way? This is a path of inner and outer work; each teacher and each school traveling the path will find helpful signposts, steep hills and deep valleys, accidental detours, and all the joys and challenges of any journey of importance.

Above all, we may strive to bear in mind the incarnating child in our care. How can we support and strengthen the child's pre-birth intention to be born in this particular body, at this particular time, in this particular place? How can we help the child to find firm ground from which to embark on his or her life's journey? In our early childhood work, we seek to bring archetypal life experiences to the children, and we might consider festivals in this light, choosing to bring each festival in its most archetypal form of uniting the human being with the earthly and the heavenly worlds—bringing a sense of the wholeness of humanity rather than a multiplicity of representations. We wish the young child to *experience* rather than to *learn about*; that will come in later years, in the rich curriculum of the Waldorf lower school and high school.

This collection of articles is offered as a sampling of various teachers' journey on the "festival path." Within the variety, we hope you will see evidence of the striving to work with the threefold curriculum mentioned at the beginning: the teacher, the developing child, and the school community. What is presented here is not intended as a definitive picture of the festival life; it is really just a beginning. We hope it may stimulate more research which might eventually result in another volume. We have chosen to focus on the cardinal seasonal festival times, leaving out other celebrations such as the Lantern Walk, Halloween, May Day, and birthdays. These additional observances might also find their way into a future collection. Because most schools are not in session at Midsummer/St. John's, we do not have any offerings on that festival. Whitsun, on the other hand, though not one of the four cardinal festivals, is included here because of its unique position as both a completion of the Easter season and a harbinger of the summer.

The book begins with a selection of articles on festivals in general, to form a basis for the sections on the seasonal festivals themselves. May you all find encouragement and renewed inspiration for your own festival work!

—*Nancy Foster*

The Cycle
of the Year

Festivals for Young Children and the Cycle of the Year

Marjorie Thatcher

*T*he Waldorf school educates children from all nationalities and religious backgrounds. Teachers are challenged to find the way to celebrate true festivals that embrace all people. The understanding of Christ as a universal being who united with both the earth and mankind makes this possible. Christ's deed was performed for all of humanity and was not limited to individuals of one religious background or another.

Throughout history and around the world, human beings have celebrated festivals. Originally, they were religious festivals connecting man with his spiritual origins and with the rhythms of nature. In the Waldorf school we mark the turning cycles of the year with the celebration of festivals.

As human beings we have a strong connection to the rhythms of nature, especially to the sun rhythm. Rudolf Steiner described the cycle of the year as a mighty breathing process. In the spring, when the earth—a living being—breathes out its forces, plant life emerges, the sap rises, and buds burst. At midsummer we feel pulled out into the light and the air. The sun is at its height and the day is at its longest at this summer solstice. Next comes the in-breathing of the forces of the earth; the plants fade and their growth ceases. By midwinter these forces are most active within the earth. The days are short, the nights long; the winter solstice is the darkest point of the year. The spring and fall equinoxes, when light and darkness are in balance, form the midpoints of these rhythms.

Young children live at an earlier stage of consciousness than adults and are deeply connected with these rhythms of nature. Watch how in summer they build tree houses, for they want to climb. In the winter they dig, finding treasures in the earth.

Festivals have always been celebrated at the four cardinal points of the year. As adults it is our task to understand what lives in the festivals in order to bring in a meaningful way what is right for the children, depending on their age. What we carry in our thinking can be put into form with the children. In the Waldorf school some of the elements of celebration are story, poetry, music, eurythmy, dancing, and drama.

On September 29, during harvest time, we celebrate Michaelmas. This festival of the Archangel Michael is an old festival, yet one that truly belongs to the future and needs to be re-created in our time as a celebration that brings awakening and courage.

The elementary school may prepare a pageant depicting the valor of St. George, Michael's earthly counterpart, as he conquers the dragon. The older kindergarten children may spend many weeks making their swords and learning how to care for them. Today, as we face the rampant "dragon" forces in our world, such a celebration prepares us to stand for what is true and good, to overcome obstacles, and to have courage in our tasks.

As the outer light of the sun diminishes in later autumn and early winter, we make lanterns, and when we carry them out into the darkness, we experience how their inner light shines forth. Then, four weeks before the Christmas festival, we come to Advent, which is a time of preparation. For the younger children we create an Advent Garden, a spiral pathway of evergreens which each child walks individually, carrying a candle. The children place the candles along the pathway until the whole Garden is aglow with light. Other traditions also celebrate festivals of light at this time of year, for example, Hanukkah, Diwali, and Santa Lucia Day.

Advent is a time of activity: dipping candles, baking, preparing plays, and making gifts. To create the appropriate peaceful mood can be a struggle in the middle of the world's whirl of events.

Advent culminates at Christmas with the birth of the Child. How the children respond to the stories of this event! The gift is given in the night, hence the traditions of Father Christmas and Santa Claus. The twelve days of Christmas are a special time and mark the turning point of the year. On January 6 comes the visit of the three kings. We can understand the Child who was born for all mankind as an archetype for the birth of every child. And each Christmas we can prepare to receive what can be born in every human soul.

After Christmas and the winter season, the earth slowly awakens with new plant and animal life. With ancient symbols—eggs and animals—we celebrate this return of life at Easter. The Easter celebration is one of early morning, of sunrise, and it is then that gifts are sought.

As we move toward midsummer, we rejoice in the blossoming world. We plan picnics and outdoor events. Community events connect us with each other at the point of the summer solstice. The St. John's Festival on June 24 is celebrated with a bonfire. It is a time for adults to burn their dissatisfactions and children their grumpiness.

Try to picture a year without festivals. How empty it would be! Without festivals we would become strangers on the earth. A living celebration of festivals is one of the most important gifts we can give our children. To create festivals is a challenge, but one that can be met joyfully in community.

᠀᠐

Marjorie Thatcher taught kindergarten, preschool, and parent/child classes at the Vancouver Waldorf School for twenty-nine years. She is a co-founder and co-director of the Waldorf Early Childhood Training offered by the West Coast Institute for Studies in Anthroposophy in British Columbia, in which she teaches classes on the festivals. She is very grateful for the rich experience of festivals in her childhood. This article previously appeared in the Bulletin of the Vancouver Waldorf School.

Festivals of the Year

Joan Almon

*A*growing question in Waldorf kindergartens and schools is to what extent Waldorf education is an expression of Christianity as a world religion or to what extent it is more broadly universal. Searching for the answer leads us towards the modern mysteries, for Waldorf education is centered around the Christ as a universal being who has helped humanity and the earth in their development from the beginning of time. Rudolf Steiner, the founder of Waldorf education, speaks of the Christ in the present time as dwelling in the etheric world surrounding the earth. The etheric world has much to do with the life forces of the earth, with nature and its seasons.

The Christ's presence, imbued with love and compassion, is felt more and more by human beings upon the earth, but it is a presence that is not limited to individuals of one particular religious persuasion. Waldorf education strives to create a place in which the highest Beings, including the Christ, can find their home, but it is not affiliated with one religion or another. For this reason one can find Waldorf kindergartens and schools in countries linked with all the religions of the world, yet all these schools feel themselves sharing a common understanding and approach.

The door to Waldorf education is open for all to enter, and early childhood educators have a special responsibility in representing this openness, for we are frequently the first teachers the parents come to know. Contemporary parents are often sensitive to the messages they receive as they first enter the life of the school. They want to know if this is simply another secular school, or a religious school promoting a particular religion, or a school that honors the spirit of all and nurtures the deepest and most universal elements of spirituality. Most, in my experience, are seeking the latter, and it is the festivals that most clearly communicate to parents our approach to spiritual experience and understanding.

My international work for Waldorf education took me to schools that celebrate festivals from many different religions. I found that one of the common elements was a deep relationship to the world of nature and its rhythms. On that foundation the teachers were developing a new understanding of how the spiritual and earthly elements of life interpenetrate and how this relationship manifests in the festivals.

As teachers we tend to live from season to season, from festival to festival, but it is also wonderful to carry a picture of the breathing rhythm of the year as a whole, including the way that the northern and southern hemispheres breathe together in an annual rhythm. Rudolf Steiner's *Soul Calendar* is a means of sensitizing ourselves to the inner moods of the year and our soul responses to them. Working with the current verse and relating it to the verse for the opposite time of year is one approach to the *Soul Calendar* which may develop a consciousness for the year as a whole and for its powerful rhythms as experienced in the northern and southern hemispheres at the same time.

I also found that working year after year with Rudolf Steiner's lecture series *The Four Seasons and the Archangels* deepened my appreciation of the festivals through the great imaginations alive in each of them. The pictures of how the spirit of the festivals is passed from one Archangel to another, and of how different aspects of a festival live in the two hemispheres at the same time, contributed to a view of the earth as a living, breathing being. All of this wove together in my classroom on the season table, in wool felt pictures, through changing colored cloths on tables, in the seasonal activities we did and the foods we ate, through the songs and verses of the seasons, and in the stories I chose, both fairy tales and simple nature tales, some offered as puppet plays.

Each season was a rich experience, and the high point was the festival celebration that we observed with the parents. I learned that the festival celebrations needed to be meaningful for the children, for the parents, and for me, and it was possible to create such festivals by entering more deeply into their spirit and meaning each year. I also discovered over the years that as my understanding grew deeper, the celebrations themselves seemed to grow simpler. Like a homeopathic drop which is small but potent, a well-prepared festival need not be elaborate to be meaningful to those present.

One starting point for approaching the festivals is to look outward at the ever-changing face of nature as the earth breathes in and out through the course of the seasons. The farther away from the equator we live, the fuller are these breaths, so that the contrast between winter's in-breath and summer's out-breath can be very great. In the town of Barrow, Alaska, for instance, residents see the sun rise in the afternoon in mid-November and an hour later watch it set. For the next sixty-four days they will not see the sun again. Of course, in the summer they have an abundance of sunlight, and all the growth of nature, which for most of us stretches over six or more months, is compressed into just two months.

Being used to an array of seasons and the shift from the short chill days of winter to the long dreamy days of summer, it was hard for me to imagine life near the equator where the sun rises and sets at the same time each day and the temperatures fluctuate only narrowly. Visiting Ecuador twice was eye-opening, for my Ecuadorian friends assured me they were very aware of the passing seasons and that the rhythm of the year was of great importance to them. When I asked a Waldorf kindergarten teacher how she reflected these changes on the season table, she said it was through the fruits, for during each month different fruits ripen. I have heard similar examples from colleagues in Hawaii, where seasonal changes are also present but not always obvious to the visitor. In such surroundings we can see how strongly the human being longs to experience time as an annual journey, not only as a daily or a monthly rhythm. It is wonderful that nature provides us with rhythmic changes, both quiet and dramatic, to meet this need.

There is another aspect to experiencing the yearly rhythm. We usually think of the similarities from one year to the next as the seasons unfold. We take delight and even comfort in seeing certain flowers bloom in the same spot each year. But gradually we may also develop a sensitivity to the differences between nature's work from one year to another. No two springs are ever quite the same, in part because some are warmer or wetter than others, but also because of subtler differences we may sense as we watch the seasons progress year after year. Evelyn Capel, a priest in the Christian Community, expresses this beautifully in the following passage from *The Christian Year*, which inspires a new relationship to the seasons and how they may live in us and in our classroom.

The background to the drama of human existence is the changing scenery of the earth's seasons. Winter changes to spring, spring to summer, summer to autumn, in much the same way each year. Their magical transformations can be relied upon but the wonder of the magic never grows stale with repetition. Spring has come before, it will come again, but there is a particular note, a subtle effluence, a shade of feeling in this spring that has never been quite the same before and which will haunt the expectation of next spring, though it will not be realized again. A particular season can be lost to one's experience if, in the midst of the pleasure in finding again its well-known, often repeated character, the heart does not catch the inner quality that can only be apprehended this once. It is a joy to find in spring the crocuses coming into blossom under the same tree where they have been growing for years, to catch in the height of summer the familiar scent of new-mown hay, to catch in the autumn the blue smoke of a bonfire rising past the bronzed leaves still fast in the branches and to sense in winter that tang of a clear frosty morning. Yet there is, amidst the familiar joys, the thrill of the unrepeatable element that makes each season in its own year an event of a lifetime, if only one is awake enough not to miss it.

So many elements weave together in creating a festival: our attunement to the season and the inner qualities or outward expressions of the season in that year compared to another year; our own evolving consciousness; and our relationship with the individual children and families in our class that year. All of these work together so that each festival celebration is unique, even if the stories and circles appear to be basically the same from year to year. Nature is different, we are different, and the children themselves are different. We can deepen this living approach to the festivals through our own meditative activity, through artistic work on the seasons and festivals, and through the study of written works that have grown out of Waldorf education and anthroposophy and speak of the festivals. Then the pathway through the year becomes a living journey which we celebrate with each other and dare to share with the highest spiritual Beings.

∞

Joan Almon is the director of the U.S. branch of the Alliance for Childhood. She is a former Waldorf kindergarten teacher, was co-founder of WECAN, and has worked internationally as a consultant to Waldorf educators and training programs.

The Rhythm of Life

Helle Heckmann
translated by Jean-Paul Bardou

Editor's note: *This is the first part of an article which appeared in Gateways, Fall/Winter 2001. A second part of the original article, focusing on the observance of Harvest, is included in the Autumn section of this volume.*

⌒

How do we bring to the child childhood's gifts of total acceptance, innocence, faith, and trust? For me, it has always been through life in nature, its constant changes and transformations, never the same and yet recognizable. For me, the fact of being a human being in nature, working with nature with consideration and respect, has been a means to bring to present-day children (and adults) an experience of forces that are far beyond our understanding, but that ask for our wondering. To be able to see and wonder is a driving force for life forces.

Nature celebrations and cosmic celebrations

Regardless of where we are on the earth, nature is at the base of our culture and our survival. We must adjust our existence according to the natural forces, it is deeply ingrained in us. A calling for a religious force that goes beyond all religious denomination is also present in nature. Nature's celebrations must always be an expression of the surroundings we live in.

For me, the cosmic celebrations are another element. They take place at specific times all over the earth, because they express a realm beyond the plane of nature.

Let's take Easter as an example. In Denmark, Easter joins with spring. So we mix the two aspects of celebration. A spring celebration expresses appreciation for the arrival of spring after a very dark period. We paint (a heathen custom) and we let the Easter Rabbit hide eggs that the children must find (the hare as a fertility symbol). Then we roll those eggs down a hill so that the hardboiled eggs split in two and the yolks roll out, a symbol for the release and the ascension of Jesus Christ as the being of the Sun. In that manner, we mix a celebration of nature with a spiritual celebration. It works quite well, because we blend many cultural traditions with spiritual cosmic realities. What happens on the other side of the earth? There it is fall, with the Lantern celebration as a Nature celebration, and Easter as a cosmic celebration. It means that for me in that situation (fall on the other side of the Earth), the raising of the Christ force must convey an inner enlightenment, while on the Northern hemisphere it must be an external experience, or how else can it be?

How can we practice our seasonal and cosmic celebrations so that they appear as parts of a whole instead of isolated celebrations?

I have first chosen to hold celebrations that I feel are relevant for our kindergarten—considering the cultural background of my children and the environment they come from. I have chosen a daily rhythm that builds on outdoors experience, because many of children are city children with limited movement possibilities—because of traffic, small apartments, and an indoor life based on sitting (computers, television, and so on). We have a delightful garden and beautiful surroundings (swamps, cemetery, and soccer field), although we are located only fifteen minutes by bicycle from the center of Copenhagen. It is quite natural for us to include these areas in our daily life. Every day we spend the first two morning hours outside the kindergarten. We walk twenty minutes, spend one hour at a specific place, and walk home again—simply so that the children get moving. (We have about twenty-five children from one to seven years of age. See *Nøkken: A Garden for Children*.) On our daily walk, we get an experience of the four elements: the whistling (or lack thereof) of the wind; the warmth of the sun, when it hides or comes out; the drumming of the rain or the splashing of the puddles; the changing states of the earth—wet, dry, planted or not, and so forth.

At the same time, nature makes frames around us, and it makes a big difference as to where we are in the course of the year. Each time has its own quality and each season makes us remember the previous one and look forward to the next one. Nature helps us remember prior experiences and build joy for upcoming ones. That expresses itself quite naturally in the different age phases the children go through in the six years they spend in the kindergarten.

The seasons don't start and end; they are like a wheel constantly in motion. For instance, our children always start singing Christmas songs in the late spring just before summer. They dance around spruce trees (Christmas trees) that have put forth new shoots and look just as if they had decorated themselves the way we, in Denmark, decorate them and dance around them by Christmas.

The complementary celebrations take place to a large extent at the same time as the real seasonal celebrations, and that is where all our pedagogical work lies, in the way we carry out the celebrations so that there is a context with the whole course of the year, a weaving in and out from one to the next, and yet some kind of an orderly sequence, so that the formative forces clearly shine through. The art is to understand nature as a rhythmical breath instead of a beat that ticks separate events.

❧

Helle Heckmann is the founder and director of Nøkken, a home-based child-care center in Copenhagen. She is active in teacher training in Denmark and abroad, and has served as a member of the Board of the International Association for Steiner/Waldorf Early Childhood Education (IASWECE) and of the International Birth-to-Three Working Group.

Festivals

Stephen Spitalny

Editor's note: *This is the first part of an article which appeared in* Gateways, *Fall/Winter 2002. A second part of the original article, focusing on the observance of Advent, is included in a later section of this volume.*

Festivals are a celebration of the seasons of the year and connect us to the world around us. They fall in an annual rhythm that can be strengthening to the physical body of the young child. For me, a festival celebrates the coming together of earthly and cosmic forces. Festivals create communities of human beings by celebrating the harmony of earth and cosmos, of matter and spirit. These seasonal celebrations mark the changing of light, the relation of the earth to the sun, and the connection to what is universal in the cycle of the year. Festivals can be the bearers of the spirit within the earthly seasons. They are points where earth-spirit and world/cosmic-spirit meet.

I find certain ideas from Rudolf Steiner helpful in considering how to create a festival in the classroom. These ideas guide my thinking about the greater cosmic forces at work in the four seasons. They form the groundwork for the manifestation of a given festival. In Lecture Five of *The Cycle of the Year as Breathing Process of the Earth,* Steiner described cosmic tendencies that pull the human being in certain directions at different times of the year. He spoke of the activities that then can help bring the human being into balance. Through this struggle for balance and self-development, the human being can receive guidance from the cosmos.

In the summer, the human soul tends to give itself up passively to world-happenings. The tendency is to dream out beyond the human being. To balance that tendency, the human is called upon to "Receive the Light," consciously to receive the light that is streaming toward us from the cosmos. The divine spiritual world reveals itself as moral impulses, which the human receives as enlightenment. The light is streaming spiritual wisdom down into the "I." The intellect evaporates and this wisdom-filled, moral element from outside streams in.

In the autumn, as the earth is going to sleep, the urge of the soul is to return to its inner life, to go inward. The call to the human soul is to "Look around Thee," to be awake and attentive to what is happening in the world. At this time we must strive for the knowledge to perceive the world of nature and the spiritual activity that lies behind it. We need soul courage for this striving.

In the winter, the earth has completed her in-breathing, and the human soul is thrown back to itself and threatened with inner contraction and paralysis. The tendency is for human beings to sink into ourselves, to dream within our own being. "Beware of Evil," calls the cosmos. Be aware and behold the evil; contemplate evil and the temptation of evil. Perhaps we could say that we draw back from the earth's darkness, or "beware of darkness." This mood is a polarity to "Receive the Light" of summertime. We experience a consolidation of the intellect that had evaporated in summer. At this time, we need temperance to guard ourselves against evil, to guard against a deviation from cosmic moral impulses. Can we find a balance, the middle way? Steiner described this as *Besonnenheit*, as ruling our impulses through reflective thinking, feeling and perceiving, through consciousness. This is the human being's winter task.

In the spring, the human soul's tendency is to sink into the flood of uprising nature forces. The call to the human being is to "Know Thyself," to stay connected with ourselves in this spring fevering. We can strive for knowledge of true human nature and a reconnection to our own higher nature—a connection with true morality. The call is to truly look at ourselves, to hold up the mirror, and see our weaknesses and limitations and where we have fallen away from our highest intentions.

With these thoughts in mind, I take into consideration the needs of the young child. One aspect to consider in creating a festival for kindergarten is to keep it simple. So much can be done with gesture and mood that speaks more powerfully than elaborate choreographed events. It seems important to avoid "festival indigestion," especially for the young child. Not only do we support the child, but we find it creates less stress in the adults' lives as well.

For all festivals, a mood of anticipation can be created through the planning and preparations. Including the children in the preparations allows them to experience and participate in the process of life, of the yearly cycle. Though it can also be special for the children to arrive to the magic of an already-created festival day, I mostly include the children in the room set-up and other aspects of preparation. Preparing the food and making decorations is a warming and enlivening activity for all involved. And food usually plays a part in any celebration, especially for the children. Traditions can be created that live and thrive over years, especially if we have children who are in our groups for more than one year. This also creates a sense of true anticipation in the children.

I focus on celebrating the divine spark that lives in each of us. A powerful guiding image for me is the light that streams toward us from the sun and stars, and the warmth and love into which we can transform that light. Perhaps that is the central theme around which the variations of individual festivals revolve. To me it is so important that our celebrations are so universal that no one feels excluded. I want all the families to experience inwardly that "this festival speaks to us." I want to celebrate what is universally human and universally cosmic/spiritual. The spiritual is celebrated, but not the specifically religious.

For me, kindergarten festivals celebrate divinities. Festivals for the older children often celebrate developed human beings such as saints. I leave saints for the grade school years. I celebrate only a few major festivals in my kindergarten. They include Michaelmas, Lantern Walk (not St. Martin's), Advent Garden, and an end-of-year Bridge Festival. I also celebrate each child's birthday. These are the festivals to which I invite the parents, but of course, in a sense, every day is a festival in kindergarten.

෧෨

Stephen Spitalny has been a kindergarten teacher at the Santa Cruz Waldorf School since 1989. Educated in psychology, he met Waldorf education as a parent. He is a former WECAN Board member and served as Gateways *editor for ten years beginning in spring of 2000.*

Working with the Cycle of the Year in Southwest Florida

Anne Savage

Editor's note: *This article is excerpted from Anne's 2004 master's project for the part-time early childhood teacher training at Sunbridge College. It is included here as an example of a teacher's dedication to forging a living relationship with the yearly cycle of a particular place, in order to support the children's incarnation process through a deep connection with the world of nature. As Anne explains, she moved from New England to take a teaching position in Florida, and she wondered how her work with the seasons and the festivals would change in this new environment. In a conversation, she said she did not find it necessary to alter the observance of Advent, since her customs were centered around the four kingdoms of nature during this time of preparation for the birth of the Child. Her Advent nature table did, however, reflect the particular gifts of nature found in southwest Florida: sea shells and starfish, for example, as part of the mineral kingdom, and the red berries of the pepper-bush in the plant world. At Easter, the plentiful butterflies offered a vivid image of rebirth, whereas in New England the butterflies do not emerge until much later in the spring. For those of us who live in a more temperate climate, Anne's careful yet lively observations of the cycle of the year may serve as an inspiration to look with new eyes at our own surroundings.*

∽

*W*aldorf kindergarten teachers strive always to bring to the children that which will be most beneficial to them in their process of incarnating. Rhythm is a very important aid to this process. In a Waldorf kindergarten, the activities the children engage in are completely bound up with the seasons of the year. The teachers help the children to develop a deep and living relationship with the events of the year.

We know that young children are formed by everything in their environment, not only by the human beings, but by the elements of the geography that surrounds them, including the mineral content of the land, bodies of water, and the climate. Sarasota, Florida, is located about two-thirds of the way down the west coast of Florida, right on the Gulf of Mexico. The climate is considered to be subtropical because we straddle the boundary between the tropical and the temperate latitudes. In summer, however, the climate is undeniably tropical.

When I moved from New England to southwestern Florida, I wanted to learn about my new environment and to deepen my understanding of the cycle of the year, not only out of my own personal interest, but in order to bring authenticity into my work with the children in my mixed-age kindergarten group.

We know that two processes are at work to cause the seasonal cycle, one discovered by natural science, and the other through the spiritual science discovered by Rudolf Steiner. The scientific explanation is based on the relationship of the earth to the sun. Because the earth is tilted on its axis, one hemisphere is more exposed to the rays of the sun than the other hemisphere during certain periods of the earth's orbit. In December, the northern half is pointing away from the sun while the southern half is pointing toward the sun and having its summer. The reverse is true in June.

According to Rudolf Steiner's lectures *The Cycle of the Year as Breathing Process of the Earth*, the seasonal cycle is also caused by the breathing of the earth—a process in the ether aura similar to inhaling and exhaling. This breathing process affects the earth's soul. In the springtime hemisphere, as new growth develops, the ethereal and soul forces begin to ascend out of the earth. As the earth breathes out its own ether body, ether rays from the sun can now permeate the earth's ether body and replenish its forces. From the interplay of sun beings and the earth soul there arise the major dynamics of springtime, the fertility of nature and the yearly renewal of life.

As summer approaches, the growth and fruiting processes culminate under the sun's influence. The earth now appears drowsy; a sleepiness appears in nature. Just as in sleep we leave our bodies behind, so has the earth's soul vacated its body. As the summer outbreath draws us out as well, it becomes increasingly difficult to think clearly, but our faculty for divining or intuition can function well.

As summer passes over into autumn, the sun's influence on the earth weakens, growth processes slow down, life withers. The earth spirit begins to inhale its soul forces back into its physical body. The earth begins to awaken. Then the elemental beings which were asleep high up in the atmosphere become conscious again. Thinking becomes easier and stronger and we are more centered.

As winter draws near, the inbreath is completed. The forces of the earth-soul are contained within its physical body. The elemental beings and the ethers are now concentrated below, underground. The powers of the sun have weakened. The gnomes are intensively active, moving at will through layers of rocks and minerals. The many spiritual beings which form the soul of the earth are now intensely awake and active. Our own consciousness is also intensified in the winter. It is in the activity of thinking that our ego manifests itself. In the darkness of winter the human ego feels its inner strengthening and we feel an interest in transforming our personal self. This manifests in a social urge, in a feeling for community, gift giving, communal meals, and so on. (See Adrian Anderson, *Living a Spiritual Year.*)

The extent to which this breathing process takes place at the poles and the equator determines their seasons. The polar and equatorial regions are not fully integrated into this yearly breathing, and their ethereal rhythms are thus unbalanced. When temperatures fluctuate very little, it is difficult to perceive the yearly breathing process (as Anderson notes). Here in southwest Florida this is my experience. The yearly rhythm is definitely unbalanced in favor of the summer, and the winter soul mood is very brief.

Southwest Florida is thought of as a land of palm trees, beaches, and perpetual summer. We must look more carefully here to see the continuous change and progression of nature throughout the year. It is a quiet rhythm, without the drama and the extremes experienced elsewhere. Seasonal changes are subtle. The world is always green, but the green changes from the delicate tender spring green to the full, lush summer green, to a fading and yellowing green as the days become shorter and cooler. The temperature range is narrower than it is farther north, with summer highs in the low nineties and winter lows in the high thirties. We do, however, also experience the shortening and lengthening of the days. Because we are closer to the equator the sun arcs higher. We have more sunlight and it is more intense.

The evergreen appearance of Florida is due to the many kinds of palms, conifers, and oaks. The oak leaves remain green until they fall, pushed off by the new growth. Individual species of plants seem to have their own rhythm of seed to fruit. There are sprouting, flowering, fruiting, and seed formation happening all year long, so that to the casual observer, Florida looks like endless summer.

Florida is home to many different bromeliads, or air plants, which derive their nourishment from the air instead of through a root system. Spanish moss is one of these, and it drapes trees and power lines. Children find endless uses for Spanish moss in their creative play. Many unusual (to a New Englander) species of animals are found, along with the more familiar rabbits, deer, squirrels, and raccoons. There are razorback or feral pigs, panthers, armadillos, and of course, alligators. Alligators are very common. They are found in most ponds and rivers right in town and are often in the children's imaginations.

The following is a rendering of a log I kept of monthly observations of the natural world in our immediate surroundings, particularly our school yard and Siesta Beach. It is in no way scientific or comprehensive. Rather, it reflects what the kindergarten children and I experience here as the cycle of the year.

Summer weather is tropical, very hot, very humid, with almost daily afternoon showers. Ninety percent of the yearly rainfall takes place between mid-June and mid-September. Great mounds of cumulus clouds pile up in the eastern sky during the afternoon. This cloud bank moves west to the coast, accompanied by much thunder and lightning. The rain, sometimes heavy, sometimes light, cools the air and refreshes us. Very often we are delighted by a rainbow. This is a powerful, daily rhythm in the summer. The trees and grasses turn a lush green.

As we move into August and September the oppressive heat, humidity, and daily rains continue. This is the time of year when tropical storms and hurricanes develop over the Gulf and over the Atlantic, and we can expect to experience at least a few of them. Bromeliads and ferns are in their glory now. Molds and mildews thrive, indoors and out.

Around mid-October, the temperature lowers, the humidity drops, and we begin to feel relief. Now it is comfortable to work outdoors again. We begin to prepare the vegetable garden for planting, weeding and digging the beds, spreading the compost, and laying down the mulch. Autumn is not a time for the great gathering of the harvest, but rather of preparing and planting. Oranges and grapefruits begin to show a hint of yellow in their dark green. Mangoes and papayas are ripening.

In November we have a shower of acorns from the oak trees in our play yard. Squirrels are everywhere. The wild grasses, particularly on the beach, are blooming in purple and rust. We begin to pick mangoes, star fruit, and avocadoes. Before Thanksgiving we plant all the vegetables, as well as annual herbs and flowers. The weather is mild. The heavy rains are finished but the dry season is not upon us yet.

In December the days begin to cool to the sixties. The grasses go to seed, and we especially notice the fountain grass and the sea oats along the beach. For about three weeks in this particular December, a huge amount of seaweed washed up on the beach, about two feet deep along the shoreline and about ten feet wide. It was scooped up into huge piles twice a week and then carted away (but not before we had great fun playing on them!). Now we begin picking oranges, grapefruits, and tangerines. Star fruits are still producing. We notice that the little lizards aren't as visible now. The pond is full of tadpoles.

In January the weather remains cool, with daytime temperatures in the sixties and fifties. The water in the Gulf is cold now, and we must wear shoes on our beach walks, and sweaters. The seaweed is gone, but for two weeks there were many dead fish on the beach. The coquinas, little clam-like bivalve creatures which live on the tide line and dig under the sand after each wave washes over them, have disappeared. Citrus fruit is still abundant. The seed pods of the cotton plants in our garden have split open, revealing puffs of white. It was such a delightful surprise for all of us. We harvested our entire crop, about thirty bolls. We will save the seeds for next year. In January we begin to experience the earliest signs of spring. We see that the egrets and herons visiting our pond have their mating plumage. Maple trees are blooming. The air has the soft fullness of springtime. Sea grapes are turning : the old leaves are turning red and the sprouting new growth is red.

In February, we have "fall" and spring together. The deciduous trees here all hold on to their old leaves until the new growth pushes them off. February and March is the time for raking and playing in the leaves. The days are warmer now and very pleasant. The maples, which just lost their leaves, are budding out and already have seeds. Mornings are foggy. This is the only time of year we see fog. Caterpillars are all over the passion vines. Ladybugs are everywhere. We have discovered their hatching place under the oak leaves. The orchid trees, the first of a procession of flowering trees, are in bloom. We notice flocks of birds, probably migrating north. We can have bare feet at the beach again and leave our sweaters home. The water of the Gulf is calm but still cool. In mid-February, in our local area, a strawberry festival is celebrated. It is the only harvest festival I know of here. In the garden we are picking snow peas, kale, cherry tomatoes, onions, and strawberries.

The weather is still pleasant in March, with less and less rainfall. Birds are building nests all around us. We see them picking up bits of wool left from the fleece we washed in the yard. The cardinals are back. (Where were they? Do they migrate somewhere?) We see starlings, mockingbirds, mourning doves, blue jays, sparrows, grackles, brown thrashers, and three kinds of woodpeckers. In the slash pines we have a pair of hawks. The little lizards are active again and the milkweed bugs have hatched out. The little wildflowers in the grass are beginning to bloom again: daisy fleabane, yellow chickweed, purple pipewort, white skullcap, pale peachy-yellow evening primrose, and moss verbena, to name a few. We now see more butterflies, though we do see them all year round: orange, black, and gold gulf fritillary, black and yellow zebra longwings, swallowtails, monarchs, and yellow sulphur butterflies.

By April, it has become very dry, though the weather is still mild. On the beach we see many more sandpipers which migrate through here in the spring. Beach morning glories are blooming. Several different kinds of green and blue dragonflies can be seen around the pond. The purple jacaranda trees are in bloom. Citrus trees are blooming with their sweet smells even as the last fruits are still hanging on.

In May it has again become oppressively hot and very dry. The beautiful red Royal Poinciana trees are blooming. These are large trees which produce twelve-inch-long seed pods which can be dried and used as shakers by the children. The children gather basketfuls of large pinecones from beneath the slash pines.

I have taken some of my observations and experiences of the cycle of the year here in Sarasota and attempted to transform them into imaginative material for the children. This took the form of seasonal nature tables, simple songs, poems, and gestures for circle time. These were my first attempts at this and it is in the process of continuous development. As another way of living with the cycle of the year I have begun working with Rudolf Steiner's *Calendar of the Soul* verses. I consider the work and study that I have done to be the beginning of a lifelong pursuit. I know that as my depth of understanding and experience of the significance of the cycle of the year increases, what I am able to bring to the children will only become richer. Rudolf Steiner speaks of the spiritual importance of nature experiences for human beings, and this is a guiding inspiration for my work.

Anne Savage moved in 2001 from Great Barrington, MA, to become a founding kindergarten teacher at the Sarasota Waldorf School. As a devoted gardener, Anne had raised virtually all her family's food while they were in New England. Upon arriving in Florida, she had to learn a new way of gardening, and this experience provided an impetus for her study of the cycle of the year in her new environment.

Celebrating Festivals with Young Children: Notes from a Conference

Nancy Foster

Author's note: *More than sixty early childhood educators gathered in Spring Valley in February, 2004, for a meeting sponsored by the Pedagogical Section before the East Coast WECAN Conference, to explore the nature of the festivals we celebrate with young children. I opened the meeting with a brief presentation describing qualities which might characterize festivals for the young child—celebrations which would offer the essence of each festival in a developmentally appropriate form. Following this talk, the participants took part in conversation groups facilitated by experienced teachers. Each group then shared elements of their conversation with the full gathering. Offered here is a somewhat informal summary of both the introductory presentation and the conversation reports, with the hope that this will stimulate and encourage others to continue renewing and enlivening their own work in this realm.*

The introductory remarks are indicated throughout by italics. The rest of the summary is from notes of the conversation reports as they related to the ideas presented in the talk. This article was published in Gateways, Fall/Winter 2004, and revised for this volume by the author.

Creating festivals arising out of the teacher as a reality

Werner Glas (co-founder of Sunbridge College and initiator of the first US kindergarten training) once said that we cannot rightly celebrate a festival with children unless we adults are celebrating it. Because children are imitative, we must offer something which is a reality to us; otherwise it is superficial or even false. We may ask whether the adults, in their work with the festival, are simply following tradition, or whether they are actively seeking to create something "modern" in the best sense—something that is alive and evolving. We may carry the ideal that teachers should offer to the children only what they themselves can penetrate or are striving to penetrate.

At one school, the full faculty held an in-service discussion about festivals, pondering the question, "What can we do to meet the incarnating child?" They experienced that it took courage to do this, to agree to live with the questions and forego immediate answers. They found it to be a very productive process. At another school, the faculty celebrates the seasonal Christian festivals together, with small groups of the faculty taking turns in planning the festivals. Each festival is preceded, the week before, with faculty study of a festival lecture by Rudolf Steiner, to help deepen the relationship to the festival.

It is essential for the teacher to penetrate with consciousness what she is offering to the children. Traditions may have deep meaning behind them, but they need to be re-examined, not followed out of habit. Traditions can be "made new" through our conscious work—for example, the Advent Garden (given various names by various schools). The teacher/adults need to be immersed in the experience, not intellectualize. We should make the festivals affirmations, not just adult creations. The teacher's inner work helps reduce questioning from the children.

Supporting the incarnation process

The child has chosen this time and place to incarnate according to pre-birth intentions formed with the help of spiritual beings. The birthday story gives this picture. In an image offered by one Waldorf educator, a true festival enlivens the vertical—the connection of heaven and earth— and places it into the horizontal— the social realm in which the child has incarnated. The child's "world" gradually expands from the mother's eyes to the family circle and gradually outward to include the early childhood group. The young child does not yet experience the wider world in a conceptual way. Thus it seems appropriate that the festival belong to the child's "here and now" in its connection with the heavenly realm. For example, a Michaelmas festival for the younger children might include picking and polishing apples—the here and now—and a recognition that the child's courage to climb high for the apples comes from Michael—the heavenly realm. The star in the apple also represents the heavenly realm.

Festivals are celebrations of the earth, but they also acknowledge that we seek to unite with a higher realm. They can bring a universal experience of what it means to be human. They can involve meaningful work, done in service of something higher. Multi-generational observances help the child to feel part of the social surroundings. Festivals should fit into the climate of a particular place, taking into account the life of nature and human beings in that place.

During Advent, stories and activities can reflect the relationship of the elements to the heavenly world and the birth of the child. One classroom had a nature table with a "Forest Family" with archetypal beings (family members, "professions," and so on) who came to visit the family in preparation for the birth. The image of the birth at deep midwinter is significant for the incarnating child. Some teachers call the child the "Child of Light," to indicate the heavenly connection.

Taking account of the "bodily religion of the child," who from birth to seven lives in the realm of the Father-God

The words in the Foundation Stone Meditation, "Ex Deo nascimur," indicate the realm of coming-into-being within the I of God, of living in the will forces in the "ocean-being of spirit." These words may in one sense present us with a picture of the nature of the incarnating child. They suggest the importance of wholeness for the young child. The healthy child, who lives so strongly in the will, in the limb system, feels at one with the surroundings—supported by the creative ground of the One, the Father-God. Thus for a given season we would strive to offer a festival experience with which they can unite fully, rather than a multiplicity of possibilities for experiencing the festival or the season. "Learning about" comes later in the child's development; "experiencing wholeness" belongs to the young child. We may note that devotion and reverence are experienced and expressed very differently in early childhood and in adulthood. Joy and satisfaction give a sense of wholeness, roundness. ("Lachen macht dick!"—Laughing makes one fat! —is an old saying quoted by one of our European mentors.)

In Advent, a story of birth supports these ideas. Bringing in the four kingdoms and the four elements supports the child's feeling of being at one with the world of nature. There is the feeling of the whole cosmos coming together to prepare for and greet the Child, and later, to follow the star. Too much explanation will interfere with the child's experience. The deepest educational experiences happen when we lead the children, but then stand by and silently witness.

Meaningful physical activity at a festival may be significant, expressing the bodily religion of the child. Real work activities, such as gardening, tending bees, or making maple syrup, might be considered festivals because they serve others and the work is for the good of the earth. A participatory experience, rather than a show, gets the will involved.

A festival acknowledges awareness of what the children haven't yet forgotten. The festivals may be the culmination of this acknowledgment. Festivals recognize and celebrate the rhythmic cycle of the year and are thus reassuring.

Seeking simplicity in a festival for young children

Antoine de St. Exupery, in Wind, Sand, and Stars, *wrote: "In anything at all, perfection is finally attained not when there is no longer anything to add, but when there is no longer anything to take away..." We want to avoid Waldorf sensory overload!*

In preparing the classroom for Advent, one may start simply and build up gradually. Try to determine what is *essential*; this is especially important for the younger children. Simplicity along with joy characterizes a festival for young children. Especially for Advent and Christmas, when there is so much stimulation—music, the media, commercialism—a sense of quiet simplicity is important, along with awareness of what is behind our practices. Along with the simplicity, the adults need to be inwardly active. Freya Jaffke spoke about a Michaelmas festival centered around simply polishing an apple, cutting it to reveal the star, and wrapping it beautifully for the child to take home. "Less is more."

Reflecting on the role of Christianity in the festival life of a Waldorf school

At one school, the stated intention (always spoken at Information Evenings which are part of the admissions process) is to observe the Christian seasonal festivals in a way that speaks to the universal in the human being. The understanding is that "universal" means, not including multiple religious festivals, but rather reaching deeply to find the essence of the human experience of the cycle of the year. This striving is a process. As a school, they make certain school-wide agreements, within which individual teachers are free within the classroom. For example, the name of the Advent Garden was changed, but individual teachers may use the word "Advent" in their classes if they feel it is right. In addition, individual teachers may choose to include certain non-Christian festivals if it seems appropriate for their particular group of children and parents. The hope is to create a mood of reverence in the festivals; this mood can then be carried into each family's particular celebrations, whatever their religion or culture.

Sometimes festival names have Christian connotations even though the actual festival observance may be universal in nature. It is good not to create barriers with names. In some schools, the child of Christmas is called the "Child of Light." The Christ-Being has permeated the earth; thus celebration of the seasons and the world of nature is a recognition of the Christ, whether named or not. In nature, we can find the universal. What is important is that the teacher is working with the Christ-Being inwardly, and that parents know this. It is important to know what lies behind the outward symbols. We would like to create new traditions, not everything mixed together; also, not Advent disguised underneath the winter festival.

Striving to recognize and meet the needs of parents in regard to festivals

We perceive that parents are often seeking:

- *nurturing of the soul life;*

- *information in advance about our festivals—what to expect, explanations;*

- *to perceive that we are not blindly following traditions, that we are in a process;*

- *to be respected, yet met with firmness of integrity.*

Simple pictures can be very meaningful to parents, and we can model for the parents how to create festivals with/for young children. There will probably always be a creative tension between parent wishes and our practices; this is not something one can ever "get right." Communication is the key.

Parents are hungry for spiritual observances. It is helpful to give parents in advance a written explanation of the meaning behind a festival observance and how it is geared to the young child. Let them know what picture you are bringing, especially at Advent.

One teacher offered parent evenings when parents could share with each other what they do at home with their families at festival times. She encouraged families to establish their own traditions, and urged simplicity to meet children at their level. Another teacher asked parents before school started, "How do you celebrate festivals at home?" It is important to respect the background and customs of families. If you honor other cultural celebrations, you see parallels within different religions. Another teacher holds a parent evening the week before a festival. She tells the stories and sometimes makes lanterns before the Lantern Walk. In this way parents arrive at the festival already familiar with what will be happening.

We seek to discern the balance between what the children need and the culture of the parents. How can we meet the parents, yet not compromise what we understand as the needs of the children? Having the parents involved in the *doing* may help build up community and anticipation and gives parents a way to be involved.

৩৩

Nancy Foster was a longtime teacher at Acorn Hill Waldorf Kindergarten and Nursery in Silver Spring, MD, and continues to be active in WECAN and in teacher education. She is author of Let Us Form a Ring, Dancing as We Sing, *and* In a Nutshell.

Finding the Realm of the Spirit of Humanity

Notes from lectures by Michaela Glöckler
recorded by Nancy Foster

Editor's note: The following is a report on two of the three lectures given by Michaela Glöckler at the 2006 WECAN East Coast Early Childhood Conference on "The Spirit of Humanity in Early Childhood Education"; it appeared in the Spring/Summer 2006 issue of Gateways. *It is included here because of the references to the role and nature of festivals in early childhood.*

O n Friday evening and Saturday morning, Dr. Michaela Glöckler read to us a quotation from Mahatma Gandhi:

*There are times
when you have to obey
a call which is
the highest of all,
that is, the voice of conscience,
even though such obedience
may cost many a bitter tear,
and even more,
separation from friends,
from family,
from the state
to which you may belong,
from all that you have held
as dear as life itself.
For this obedience
is the law of our being.* (1919)

This quotation was the keynote for her theme of becoming peacemakers, following our conscience as we establish a new identity with our higher Self in the realm of the Spirit of Humanity. Through the Goethean approach to the young child, we can observe the developmental steps toward the awakening of the "I." Trust is the underlying necessity for these three steps:

1. **Self-initiation into the mystery of space:** In this sacred ground of self-teaching, the child orients the self in the three dimensions and comes into the upright.

2. **Self-initiation in speaking:** The child enters into soul-to-soul communication through the vehicle of language, by means of three components: genetics, environment, and the Self. Initially the child is open to whatever language(s) are offered in the environment.

3. **Self-initiation in thinking:** There is no imitation involved in thinking; rather, the child "wakes up" to realize he has thoughts and learns to express them. To say "I" to the Self is the awakening of thinking. This "I" indicates the spiritual reality that is in all of us; I share the ability to say "I" with all of humanity. The "I am" is the Spirit of Humanity, and the child finds it out of his own striving.

The Spirit of Humanity is the crown of nature, but it is still in its infancy. Animals are wiser: they cannot be evil. Only human beings disturb the ecological balance.

We call nature divine because it is so complete. Only the human being has the possibility and the need to develop, to improve. What the human being has to learn is beyond nature; it is from the spiritual realm. For example, the infant has a walking reflex, but true walking does not arise from this reflex. The baby must overcome this reflex and develop his own walking through sensory-motor learning—that is, he must bring nature under his own will-control. As human beings, we are not the slave of our instincts.

This first experience of overcoming instinct gives us self-trust, the realization, "I can learn; I can develop." Thus the steps of development above are humanizing principles, with trust as the prerequisite.

As developing human beings, we must learn to be homeless in order to find our higher Self. In his 1910 lecture cycle *The Mission of the Individual Folk Souls*, Rudolf Steiner describes the necessity of entering consciously into our Folk Soul identity to see what it can contribute to humanity, thus also learning to see the mission of other Folk Souls. We must strengthen our ego and establish a new identity independent of the Folk.

Dr. Glöckler pointed out that babies are truly "homeless" in this sense: the younger the child, the more open and the less bound to a particular Folk Soul. Therefore, we do not want to offer a "museum of religions" in the kindergarten by celebrating festivals of every family's religion. Instead, in early childhood education we can lay the basis for an independent self-identity through keeping the realm of common humanity alive in the young child and developing a strong sense of the Spirit of Humanity. The ideal in the kindergarten is that all festivals meet the challenge to address the common Spirit of Humanity.

The elements of such festivals might be the following:

- admiration of nature, a spiritual relationship to the laws of nature;

- the magic of the social aspect—the joy of preparing a festival for one another;

- living with threshold experiences, making thresholds conscious, in a manner appropriate for specific developmental stages.

Without the spiritual in education, children would be cut off from the source of their humanity, yet religion is a private matter. What we bring into the early childhood classroom must be that which is beyond a personal religion. Rudolf Steiner said that Christianity began as a religion but has become something more. By bringing it into the thought realm, it transcends the sectarian. In *How to Know Higher Worlds*, we find concepts from many religions, because Rudolf Steiner was seeking to formulate a universally human path of development so that nearly any human being could participate. "There slumber in every human being faculties by means of which he can acquire for himself a knowledge of higher worlds." This idea that each human being can find the spirit is also found in the Gospels. (Religious traditions often do not reflect this; we have to go to the source.)

Dr. Glöckler ended by giving a picture of human nature in the context of the challenge of the adversarial beings. In the Old Testament, there are two creation stories. In the first, the human being is portrayed as a spiritual being, encompassing all realms, and is declared by God to be "very good." In the second, the human being is portrayed as a physical being, with each kingdom of nature placed beside the others. Here, there is the possibility of evil. The very young child belongs with the first picture. Once ego-consciousness has dawned, the second picture is added, and so we have both possible views of our humanity.

The anthroposophical understanding of this paradox is found in the qualities of Lucifer and Ahriman. Lucifer represents the ancient paradigm of fanaticism: "You will know what is good and what is evil." This ignores the reality that good and evil are in all of us, and denies the possibility of development, of becoming.

Ahriman intends that we forget good and evil and view the human being as an animal which can be formed and directed. This is the modern paradigm, in which freedom is seen to cause trouble and human beings are treated as automatons.

Our challenge is to develop moral intuition, the ability to discern in the moment what is good or evil. We must not fall into either of the above paradigms, but find our way forward as human beings on a path of development to the realm of the Spirit of Humanity. Another verse from Gandhi speaks to us of strength of heart and the power of everlasting spirit:

Power invariably elects to go
into the hands of the strong.
That strength may be physical
or of the heart,
or, if we do not fight shy
of the word, of the spirit.
Strength of the heart
connotes soul force.
Let it be remembered that
physical force is transitory.
But the power of the spirit
is permanent even as
the spirit is everlasting. (1942)

৶

Michaela Glöckler is currently the head of the Medical Section at the Goetheanum in Dornach, Switzerland. She has been active as a pediatrician and school doctor in Germany and is the co-author with Wolfgang Goebel of A Guide to Child Health, *Floris Books.*

Autumn:
Harvest Time and
Michaelmas

Celebrating the Harvest

Freya Jaffke

Editor's note: The following is a summary of a talk given by Freya Jaffke at a kindergarten course in England. The notes were taken by Gale Ramm of Michael Hall School and were reviewed by the lecturer. Many teachers find a deep connection between Michaelmas and the harvest (see, for example, the story "Michael and the Dragon" in this volume), so it seems appropriate to include this in the section on Michaelmas.

*T*he child is not able to look over a long period of time as an adult can and therefore needs an outer sign to spark its memory. "It was like this last year," the child will say. The child lives in the present, totally a sense being, a being of will. We can observe this in the way the child acts, always taking in some impressions and working out these impressions in its will, with the gift of imitation which the child has brought to earth.

Our guiding word should be *doing...doing...doing*, never reasoning *why* something is done in a certain way, although sometimes children have their own philosophy about certain things. Our task as kindergarten teachers is to try to transform everything we do, to transform our knowledge into activities: to make visible that about which we have been thinking. As a human being we have a strong connection to the natural surroundings and to the seasons. Our connection to the festivals, however, is not so immediate, and we have to think about them if we want to include more than just traditions in our celebrations. Let us explore the festivals from summer to midwinter.

The mood of high summer is one of devotion to the light. We go outdoors and leave our houses; we want to be outside to experience all the manifestations of nature occurring at this time: the scent of flowers, the warmth of sun and air. We go on holidays to the sea. After St. John's tide, the breathing-in process begins. This is the time of ripening. The first fruits of summer, the berries, are ripe. The grains also ripen in the fields. Passing through the threshold of autumn, we come to winter, at which time the soul of the earth is taken in most deeply. How the human soul follows these processes, but in a different way, is the subject of what is to follow.

The first festival we come to is the Harvest Festival, a time of thanksgiving. Remembering that our thoughts have to be visible in our deeds, how can we express thankfulness in everyday life? The kindergarten needs caring for. This happens all the time, of course, but now we can harvest everything in the garden. Herbs can be dried, stripped from their stalks, the brown leaves sorted from the good, put into bags or jars to be used later for tea. Flowers for drying can be gathered and dried and stored in bags or jars.

How we do this is important—not in a hectic way but with an inner thankful attitude and with joy, keeping in one's mind the fact that we receive gifts from nature and that we know how to use these gifts. The leaves and other treasures which the children collect can be placed on the seasonal table. The children like to see how they change as they dry. It is important that there is a place in the kindergarten where these things are honored and treasured.

And we may speak about and name the four grains: oats, wheat, barley and rye, and use them! (**Editor's note:** *In North America we also use corn, rice, and millet, grains which are associated with the Americas, Asia, and Africa, respectively.*) Much later in their school years the children will come to know the concepts about the grains; in the kindergarten it is sufficient to know their names. A harvest wreath can be made with the grains and hung inside or can be hung outside for the birds. The children may help to make the wreath by handing their teacher the small bunches of grain to be tied on. In a parents' evening it is possible to speak about this time of year and the details of the upcoming festival. Freya Jaffke described her festival in the following way:

On the festival day each child is asked to bring a little basket filled with autumn fruits and vegetables from their surroundings. Their baskets are placed on a table in the middle of the kindergarten room. In the center of this table can be placed a harvest loaf baked especially for this festival and which is surrounded by flowers and candles. We need to think how to celebrate the festivals with many healthy sense impressions with which to nourish the children.

The festival begins with the rhythmical harvest circle games which have been played with the children since the beginning of the school year. These games have to do with the processes of harvesting, threshing, and milling of the grain, with the baking of the bread, and with the gathering of the fruit from the orchard, and so on. On this occasion the parents join in the circle games with the children.

Afterwards, everyone, including smaller children who come to the festival, as well, sit in a large circle around the harvest table. The curtains are closed, the candles are lit, and grace is said:

Earth who gives to us this food,
Sun who makes it ripe and good,
Dearest Earth and dearest Sun,
We'll not forget what you have done.

—Christian Morgenstern

The harvest bread is then shared and afterwards some of the fruits from the children's baskets are also shared. At a suitable time, the candles are snuffed out.

Looking back at the festival, there has been no word about being thankful but everything has been done in an attitude of thankfulness. There have been many sense impressions including the colors of the flowers and fruits and the light of the candles. This festival takes place at the end of September or the beginning of October.

∽

Freya Jaffke is now retired after many decades of work as a Waldorf kindergarten teacher and teacher trainer in southern Germany. She has lectured and mentored Waldorf kindergarten teachers widely throughout the world. Her books on early childhood have sold over a quarter of a million copies worldwide.

The Harvest Observance

Helle Heckmann
translated by Jean-Paul Bardou

Editor's note: *This is the second part of an article, "The Rhythm of Life," which appeared in* Gateways. *The first part, urging us to consider the seasons of the year as "a wheel constantly in motion" and nature as "a rhythmical breath instead of a beat that ticks separate events," is offered in the "Cycle of the Year" section of this publication.*

〜

T o start with harvesting time is like going directly to the end of a good book. At harvesting time we harvest our diligence! On the outside, we harvest the crops given to us by the earth, depending on how well we have done at reading nature, at sowing in a timely manner and at taking care of our crops.

For me, harvesting grains is an archetypal experience. I still ask myself whether it is not a bit artificial to bring my city children to the countryside and see a farmer harvest with a scythe and gather sheaves to bring them back to the kindergarten. Nowadays children know that all this is done with huge machines and they cannot connect a scythe with a grain field (if they have seen one in the first place). Anyway, I still stubbornly keep the farm visit for all families as a shared outing and a sensory experience because I see some archetypal movements in the sweeping of the scythe through the grain and in the sound of the meeting between scythe and grain. As we stand outside in the field, we hear the wind, the sky is high above, and we can see far on every side. To have seen the farmers' genuine movements makes it also possible to make the right movements during song games. I think that it is very important to be able to imitate the proper movements.

After the farm visit, we take about fourteen days to "harvest." The grain stands in sheaves in the garden to be seen and to be touched. We sing harvest songs, and after a couple of days, we thresh the grain. All children stand in a circle and as we sing the harvest songs we go around the small harvest sheaves. When we get to the part of the song that says: "Do you know how the farmer threshes…" we all bend down, take a sheaf and thresh the grain from the ears on the white sheet that lies in the middle. We repeat that threshing motion time after time, some children with great care, some with a lot of force, while others simply watch (the small ones are sleeping at that time). Seeing the grain jump out of the ears is magic that is commented on with excitement. When all the bundles have been threshed, two adults grab an end of the sheet, as the children stand off to the side; *one– two–three—*

we throw grain and chaff in the air. The wind will blow the chaff away and the grain falls back, nice and clean into the sheet. To feel grain is a blissful experience—"Me too!" "Me too!"—all the children stream by and bury their hands in the heap of grain, a special moment.

After that the small hand-driven grain mills come out and the children take turns grinding (we have about seven mills for sixteen children). For days, they grind and grind to make flour during the afternoon hours. On our morning outings, we bring the straw, which we adults—helped or watched by the children—make into wreaths and various braided objects. We sing as we work. This is an industrious time.

Harvest work takes place all over the garden. Fruit, berries, and vegetables must be harvested—at different times, though—and they must be processed or dried. Flowers must be watered, animals must be fed, and rabbits must be shorn. It is a time with lots of work to do. We round it off with a harvest celebration to which the parents, who bring homemade cakes, are invited from 1:00 p.m. to 2:30 p.m.

We have baked bread and prepared elderflower juice (from before the summer vacation) so that we are reminded of the days before summer, when everything had a different color and the atmosphere was different. On the day of the celebration, we go to a special place where we churn cream into butter in jam jars and bring it back home. We then dress with festive clothes; all the children have brought special fine harvest clothes (by "fine," I don't mean new or expensive, but clothes they connect with special times, celebration, and joy). We all comb our hair and admire each other under this transformation. We shed the old and renew ourselves.

In a long line, we go to the kindergarten room, which has been decorated for the occasion with harvest sheaves, rosehips, wild flowers, and so on. We sit by a long table and today the children get to butter their own bread, decide themselves what they will have on their bread, and kindly ask to be handed this or that. There is abundance; many children get their fill just by looking.

After that comes the harvest story. It is told out in the garden, among the fruits and vegetables the children have brought themselves the day before. One of the pedagogues has prepared a story on the theme: The king invites people to a harvest celebration, because the princess wants to get married...The children are as quiet as mice. After the story, it is time to play in the garden, where children can repeat the story or invent new ones, or simply play in peace and quiet. The adults are busy in the garden, preparing the tables for the parents' visit.

When the parents arrive, they wait in the garden by the entrance of the kindergarten (and deliver the cakes). When all have arrived, we go in a singing chain to the garden towards a pile of straw. There the parents sit and weave a light wreath or take up another task. It is important that the parents have something to do. During that time, the children play around in the garden, and the parents can catch a glimpse of children at play.

After half an hour, all are invited to the tables and we sing our mealtime song. Then we eat and we chat. All get a beautiful wreath to take home, to be hung by the entrance door or on a wall, or to be laid on a table to be decorated again with various flowers. In any case, the wreath is kept until Advent Spiral time, at which time it is brought back to be transformed into an Advent wreath with spruce branches from the spiral. In that manner, harvest time and the Advent spiral time mesh with one another, with Michaelmas and the Lantern celebration in between.

ରଡ

Helle Heckmann is the founder and director of Nøkken, a home-based child-care center in Copenhagen. She is active in teacher training in Denmark and abroad, and has served as a member of the Board of the International Association for Steiner/Waldorf Early Childhood Education (IASWECE) and of the International Birth-to-Three Working Group.

St. Michael on the Crescent of the Moon

From a Polish Legend

Editor's note: *This beautiful story is found in the collection* Michael Legends—The Deeds of Michael: A Collection of Tales and Legends, *available in typescript from the Rudolf Steiner Library in Ghent, NY. Although this tale is not appropriate for young children, it can serve as an inspiration to us as adults, and in fact inspired the story by Bella Schauman included in this section.*

Hast thou seen gleaming, on clear and exalted nights, the sparkling stars in the sky? They rise like hope in a human soul; they dive down in radiant force, like a human heart's resolve. Then they are called falling stars by men.

But whoever loves his angel, and from childhood on, knows no fear, recognizes their true being. He sees in the clear autumn nights amidst the stars the great warrior who is called St. George on earth and St. Michael in the heavens. And he sees his countenance shining in golden wisdom; a countenance which, unconscious of itself, reflects the heart of the highest Godhead. And he sees his arm with the shimmering weapon which, strong and pure, seems to be hardened by Divine Justice.

And with his valiant hand, St. Michael strikes the sword, which will destroy the crawling, the desirous, the wallowing, the corroding impurity. And when St. Michael strikes his sword, the stars tremble and diamantine sparks fly through the air.

Hast thou seen gliding, in dark winter nights, the delicate moon crescent above the gossamer white clouds? There is around them something like a rustling of distant grass growing on the wide and fair meadows of Heaven. The hearts of men looking at the crescent in wintry nights are seized by a longing to be far, far away.

But whoever loves his angel, and from childhood on, has harbored purity in his heart, sees something else. He sees the Heavenly Virgin, Maria, standing on the narrow silver crescent. And he knows that she is a Queen. For she smiles at those who are longing and hungering on earth. And she bestows on them heavenly wheat-grains which fall down from her rosy hands and bring blessings to earth. She prays that the depths may become filled and may become good and may become penetrated with the miracle harbored in the heights. She bestows blessings with hands that are folded in prayer.

And one day it will happen that the birch tree, when its leaves are falling in autumn, will not weep because of its bereavement. Then the leaves will joyously fall down to earth. And Maria, waving her hands in a promise of redemption, will walk up the white steps unto the golden table spread in heaven with the thanksgiving of men on whom the harvest has been bestowed. And it seems as if her foot were treading on fluttering doves' wings.

Henceforth the moon's crescent will not be forsaken. A song will resound from it, such as has never been heard in Heaven and on Earth. St. Michael will stand on the crescent. As a heavenly smith, he has forged his sword into the frame of a lyre whose strings are fashioned from men's valiant thoughts. The dragon slayer will play and sing. He will perform his office as heavenly lutist. Strength is alive in his song. He will sing of consolation and fulfillment of old promises. He will sing of the outflowing of the highest light encompassing the smile of Maria.

And the birch tree will tremble down to its very pith in its joyfulness, whenever this song is sounded. And autumn will be the same to it as spring.

Many a man will not see it, many a man will not hear it. But whoever loves his angel and harbors faithfulness in his heart: such a one knows the song full well and will want to be better.

෨ඏ

The original work is in German: Aus Michaels Wirken: eine Legendensammlung, *Stuttgart [Germany]: J.Ch. Mellinger, 1977, c1959, by Nora Stein von Baditz, with an introduction by Ita Wegman and a contribution from Herbert Hahn. The story "Sankt Michael auf der Mondsichel" appears on p. 91.*

Images of Michaelmas

Nancy Foster

Editor's note: *This article was originally written for the newsletter of Acorn Hill Waldorf Kindergarten and Nursery. It is included here to illustrate one way of including parents in a growing understanding of the festivals of the year.*

*I*n a temperate climate such as ours, the seasons of the year carry us through time in a predictable, reassuring rhythm. In autumn we rake leaves and prepare a Thanksgiving meal; in winter we wait for the first snowfall and take our children sledding; in spring we rejoice at the first crocus bloom and unpack our warm-weather clothing; in summer we let the children play in the sprinkler and we escape the heat at the beach or in the mountains. The world of nature provides a framework for our lives. This framework is often filled out by a particular family's religious or cultural traditions. For all of us, recognition of the spiritual world's role in the realm of nature and in the lives of human beings brings a sense of reverence to our experience of the yearly cycle.

At Acorn Hill, much of our life in the classroom rests on this same framework of the course of the year. Soon after school begins, we enter the season of Michael (often pronounced "Micha-el" to remind us of its derivation from the Hebrew: "who is of God"), the Archangel who was the protector of the ancient Hebrew people and who brings us strength to face the powers of darkness within and around us. Michaelmas, beginning on September 29, is associated with harvest time and the approach of winter. In the England of older times, it was at Michaelmas that harvest workers were hired for the following year's work.

This is the season when we must strengthen ourselves for the months of cold and darkness to come, bearing within us the light and warmth that were in the outer world of nature in summertime. It is also the time when we must be inwardly awake to the quality of our thoughts and deeds, weighing them in the balance scales often pictured in old paintings of the Archangel Michael.

The qualities of courage and inner light which belong to the autumn season of Michael are an essential element of the experiences we bring to your children at Acorn Hill. The images which appear in songs, verses, and stories are many; we select those most appropriate for the age of the children in our groups. Some of the classes may hear a story of Michael and the dragon, based on a Polish harvest legend. Some will sing songs or move to verses about Michael. Many of the children will help to thresh wheat, a harvest activity which creates another image of awake judgment: "separating the wheat from the chaff."

Another image of the Michaelmas season is the apple. As the children wash and polish the rosy apples, they experience the strong red of courage, and the quality of shining light which we seek at this time of year. And—a wonderful mystery—in the center of each apple is a five-pointed star, which we can imagine as a picture of the human form standing with arms and legs outstretched. The star is also a symbol of light, and may remind us that strength and light come from the starry heavens to help us find these qualities in our own lives. The meteor showers of late summer contribute to this sense of heavenly gifts.

These images associated with Michaelmas are to be pondered by us as adults. It is important to remember, though, that for our young children it is the *experience* of these images and activities that is meaningful, and it would be inappropriate to try to explain the underlying thoughts and concepts. In time, the children's experiences will ripen into an understanding that will be truly their own.

Nancy Foster was a longtime teacher at Acorn Hill Waldorf Kindergarten and Nursery in Silver Spring, MD, and continues to be active in WECAN and in teacher education. She is author of Let Us Form a Ring, Dancing as We Sing, *and* In a Nutshell.

Taming the Dragon:
Michaelmas in the Kindergarten

Barbara Klocek

Editor's note: This article, and the Michaelmas Circle which follows, offer an example of an experienced teacher's search for a meaningful, satisfying way to bring the experience of Michaelmas to a mixed-age kindergarten group. Both appeared in the Spring/Summer 2001 issue of Gateways, *and were revised for this volume by the author.*

How can we find the right imagination to bring to young children in observing the festival of Michaelmas? For many years I have lived with this question. I work in a mature school which has rich traditions for this festival.

A large dragon is constructed by the sixth grade class, so large that they all fit inside. At the festival, the third grade class is dancing a harvest dance when the dragon arrives. But behold, Michael appears (a carefully chosen twelfth grader) and, supported by verses recited by classes two through twelve, subdues the dragon in a gesture with his sword.

Our kindergarten often included a story of George and the Dragon and the making of wooden swords, but I was a strong pacifist and struggled with the idea of arming the children, even if it was to overcome the dragon. As a mother of three sons, I had for many years focused on non-violence and peace, but I found I was meeting a very strong counter-stream within my boys that needed understanding. For a while I became a militant pacifist but then saw that this counter-stream was a dynamic with which I needed to work.

When I first became a kindergarten teacher, I searched for different, gentler images and activities to bring to my class for Michaelmas. I found many wonderful stories in the Wynstones *Autumn* book and through conversations with wise teachers. Working with wood, rasping, sawing, drilling, and polishing, was a wonderful activity in the kindergarten, and I found the older boys were especially satisfied, but I was not at ease with the swords.

So one year we made golden capes instead, dyed from the gold gathered in the drying of our marigolds. I told a gentle story about Michael leading the star children across the stormy sea. This was beautifully suited to the younger children; however, upon reflection that year, I saw a certain restlessness in the older boys. The need for the archetypes of the hero who conquered the evil and of the knight who was brave and true had not been met. The emerging will of these young boys was seeking resistance, needing to tame the dragon.

We see this need for resistance on the playground as these young boys delight in pushing against the density of the earth in the sandbox or digging a hole. They need to engage their will in transforming substance. So I began to look at the sword in a new way. I created a circle (following) that would give images in which to understand and transform the role of the sword.

I still choose the Michaelmas story with care, rewriting the story of George and the Dragon or finding a simpler story if my class is young. And we have continued to make the silk capes. I have come to see that in our time the children need the cape of light to give them courage and strength. From the gathering and drying of the petals of the marigolds early in the school year, to the days just before Michaelmas, this has proved to be a wonderful activity. We stir the petals in a big pot and it simmers all day. The next day we drain the mixture through cheesecloth, and each child gets to dye a cape. These are 35-inch square silk scarves for a very reasonable cost.

The children love this project. One girl commented, "We put the white silk in the dark water and it comes out gold." The capes look so lovely as they dry on the line outside the class. After they are finished by ironing, each child receives one on Michaelmas with the words, "I give to you a cape of light, to give you courage, strength, and might." This is a line from the Michaelmas play which takes place during story time.

In addition, I have returned to the making of wooden swords with the older children. If the younger children want to work on a sword they can work on two or three extra swords that then become the class swords. The children spend several weeks sanding, first the long piece and then the crosspiece. We sometimes begin with homemade sandpaper that we make with heavy paper, white glue, and sifted sand from the sandbox. Gradually we get to the fine, store-bought sandpaper. Finally we cut pegs from a dowel and drill the hole to join the two notched pieces together. We hammer in and glue the peg and then paint the swords a beautiful gold with our watercolors. They dry overnight and are then sanded with the finest sandpaper and oiled, with a red yarn tie at the crosspiece. They are then placed carefully on the nature table where they remain until Michaelmas, except for use in the Michaelmas play.

At the end of our Michaelmas celebration day, each child receives her cape of light to take home. The children who have made a sword are given it with the words (from the circle), "You have polished your sword so strong, so bright. Use it only for the right." I also give the parents a copy of part of the verse and ask their help in keeping this mood at home for the sword. This imagination lives within the class for the whole year. One year when I went to put away the Michael puppet the children asked where he was. They have been delighted and satisfied that he now lives near the morning candle. The older boys carry the imagination of Michael into free play, and one feels a strengthening of their resolve to be courageous, to subdue the dragon, and to serve the right.

❧

Barbara Klocek has been a kindergarten teacher at the Sacramento Waldorf School for many years. She holds an M.F.A. in fine arts and has worked as an art therapist. She has raised three sons and loves music, nature, and art. With her husband, she tends a bountiful garden.

Michaelmas Circle

Barbara Klocek
(Gateways, Spring/Summer 2001)

Editor's note: *This is the circle mentioned in Barbara's article, "Taming the Dragon: Michaelmas in the Kindergarten." The songs and verses are from oral tradition and other sources.*

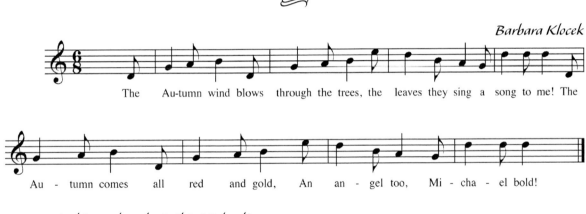

Barbara Klocek

The Au-tumn wind blows through the trees, the leaves they sing a song to me! The Au - tumn comes all red and gold, An an - gel too, Mi - cha - el bold!

And I wonder who is this Michael?
And I hear the wind sing:

Barbara Klocek

Mi - cha - el, God's great knight, strong and pure and shin - ing bright.

I'll be a knight of Michael, too,
And polish my crown to a golden hue.
Ask the gnomes the iron to mine,
Iron from the stars, from the earth, so fine,
To bring to the blacksmith, who with his might
Will make me a sword, so strong, so bright.

And we follow the falling stars to the mountain cave where the gnomes are working.

And the gnomes say:

With fire and stone, we work with a will
With our strength and our skill.
The iron we soften and then we bend
Into hammers, swords, and nails to mend.
Dear gnomes, may I have some iron?
Are you noble? Oh, yes.
Are you good? Oh, yes.
And do you hear the singing of the stars? Oh, yes.
Then you may have some iron.

Barbara Klocek

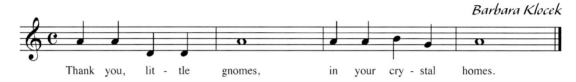

Thank you, lit - tle gnomes, in your cry - stal homes.

Oh bring me a galloping horse for to ride,
A crown on my head, the iron by my side.
Off to the blacksmith we must go.
Galloping, galloping, off we go.
Dear blacksmith, will you make me a sword?
Of course! for:

traditional Dutch

I am a black-smith good and true, Best of work I al-ways do, All ___ day

long my ham - mers go, Cling-ing, cling-ing, clang-ing so, A-rick-et-y dick-et-y dick-et-y

dick, A-rick-et-y dick-et-y dick-et-y dick, A-rick-et-y dick-et-y dick-et-y dick.

Thank you, kind blacksmith, for your might.
I'll polish my sword, so fine, so bright.
I will use it for the right,
Not for some silly quarrel or fight,
But to drive away evil, I will try
And protect those who are weaker than I.

(After a week or two of the preceding, the following is added.)

Oh bring me a galloping horse for to ride,
A crown on my head, my sword by my side,
For it's off to the castle we will go.
Galloping, galloping, here we go.

The knights came together and proclaimed:

No fear here! Michael, be my guide and stand by my side.
And they knew that Michael was always ready to help.

(During the song, teacher kneeling in the center tosses a bean bag star to each child.)

Barbara Klocek

Mi-cha-el,   God's great knight,   strong and pure and   shin-ing   bright.   Fall-ing star

in   the   sky,   Give   us   strength   to   keep ___ us   by.

And we are always guarded by Michael.

Barbara Klocek has been a kindergarten teacher at the Sacramento Waldorf School for many years. She holds an M.F.A. in fine arts and has worked as an art therapist. She has raised three sons and loves music, nature, and art. With her husband, she tends a bountiful garden.

Michael and the Dragon

Adapted from a Polish tale by Nancy Foster

Author's note: *This story is intended for a mixed-age kindergarten group.*

O nce, long ago, in a far-off land, there lived a King who ruled his country kindly and well.
It was a beautiful country, and a prosperous one, for the farmers took good care of their
land. Each year on a certain day, when the wheat stood tall and golden and was ready for
harvesting, the people put on their gayest clothes, and brought their gifts of ripe fruits and vegetables
to the King. Now the King had one beautiful daughter, and it was her greatest pleasure on this special
day to stand out on her balcony and watch the joyful procession coming to the palace.

One year, however, it happened that the people came empty-handed. They looked very sad, and
walked along with their heads bowed down. The King spoke to them, saying, "My beloved people,
why do you not bring your harvest gifts?" "Alas," said the people, "we have no gifts to bring. Indeed,
we shall not have enough food to eat this winter. Our families will go hungry; for a fearful dragon with
fiery breath has come to our land and has burned up all our crops with his breath."

Then the King declared, "I will send all my bravest knights to fight this dragon." The knights
went out to meet the dragon, but their swords just melted in the fire from his breath. Then the King
sent a messenger to the dragon, to inquire what treasure they might offer him, so that he would leave
their country. But the dragon replied, "No, keep your treasure! I do not need it; I have what I like.
Instead, you must give me the King's daughter."

When the messenger returned to the King and told him that the dragon required his daughter,
the King wept. "No," he said, "I would gladly give the dragon all the royal treasure, but let me keep my
daughter."

But the King's daughter heard her father speaking, and she came to him, saying, "I will go to the
dragon, Father. I am not afraid. I know that the heavens will watch over me."

And so the King had his daughter dressed in the purest white, and he kissed her and gave her his blessing, and let her go. He watched her sadly as she walked to the hill to meet the dragon, holding her head high. The knights accompanied her for a time, but when they reached the hill where the dragon was, they stayed behind and the King's daughter went on alone.

As the princess began to climb the hill, the dragon suddenly appeared, breathing his fiery breath. At that very moment, a heavenly light streamed from above. The heavens opened, and Michael stepped forth with his arm outstretched. In his hand was a sword—not an ordinary sword, but a heavenly sword, forged from the stars.

Michael pointed his sword at the dragon, and at that instant the dragon fell to the earth, overcome. Then there was a great celebration. The knights led the princess back to the palace in a grand procession, and the people rejoiced. When the farmers went back to their homes, they found their cellars full of the finest fruits and vegetables, and plenty of grain ready for the mill. And so it was that each year, from that time on, at harvest the people celebrated a festival of thanksgiving to Michael, who saved their crops from the dragon.

෧෨

Nancy Foster was a longtime teacher at Acorn Hill Waldorf Kindergarten and Nursery in Silver Spring, MD, and continues to be active in WECAN and in teacher education. She is author of Let Us Form a Ring, Dancing as We Sing, *and* In a Nutshell.

Michaelmas in the Nursery: A Celebration of Courage

Carol Grieder-Brandenberger

Editor's note: *This article, part of Carol's 2008 master's project for the Sunbridge Part-time Early Childhood Training, is written from her perspective in the spring, looking back at the beginning of the year and at the children who entered the nursery class on the first day of school. Her experience of their deed of courage led her to consider the significance of Michaelmas in a most direct way in the life of the young child.*

⤿

Way up high in the apple tree
Two red apples looked down at me.
Along came the rain and shook that tree,
Down came the apples, just for me.

The season of Michaelmas lies between midsummer and winter. From times past, the Archangel Michael has been given a variety of attributes: hero of the sun, lord of harvest, helper of human beings, protector of the globe and of the ability to decide between good and evil. According to an ancient legend, Michael holds a sword of light with which he can ward off the dragon. In *Festivals with Children*, Brigitte Barz describes Michaelmas as a tide or season that lasts four weeks. She states that the task of the Archangel Michael is to infuse humanity with the power to recognize and experience the spirit and allow it to become effective in human deeds. Rudolf Steiner describes the majestic picture of Michael with the flaming sword of iron in battle with the sulphurous dragon as an inspiring impulse for what we must become if we are to develop the forces of our evolution for progress and not for decline.

It is helpful for the teacher to carry the awareness that also in the lives of our three- to four-year-old nursery children, dragons exist. And there is a way in which the children stand up to the dragons. Once we teachers have put all our energies into the preparations for the first days of school, and once the parents have put all *their* energy into preparing for the separation, it is the children who make the step into the new world of an early childhood group. Even with all the support of their loved ones and teachers, they make this step alone. It fills me with awe, thinking of all the children who on the first day of school cross over the bridge into the nursery after saying goodbye to their parents. Certainly, this is a true Michaelic moment.

So the question arises: How can we celebrate this moment? How do we celebrate the season and give tribute to the strength and courage which the children carry within?

One of my mentors emphasized to me how important it is for the teacher to carry the festival within herself. This in itself is so important that it will lead to a celebration of the festival, even without many planned festivities. In the nursery, I feel that by holding within me the image of Michael facing the dragon, I am honoring the dragons which the children are facing as they start school, often for the first time.

Since the season of Michaelmas is also the season of harvest, it appears that the two are often combined. In fact, Michael has been depicted in one of his aspects as the lord of the harvest, who stands at the threshold from summer to winter in the mood of autumn. I found a very simple harvest circle play meaningful, starting with only a few elements and gradually adding to them. To honor the season, I told the well-known story, "The Turnip." It speaks about harvest, and also about the importance of every person who is needed to finally pull out the giant turnip. Only after the mouse helps can the turnip be harvested. Every child, even the smallest, is important in the nursery. Every child is needed.

"The Turnip" is a nature tale as well as a traditional folk tale. It is simple enough for the three-year-old children in a nursery or mixed-age kindergarten and can be told with puppets and repeated many times. For the nursery children, it is good to have the story told as a puppet show, as it helps them create inner pictures to accompany the words.

During the week of Michaelmas, I offered the Michaelmas table play, "George and the Apples," by Cecilia Karpoff (found in this volume). In its lovely rhymes I told the story of the boy who climbs the tree, picks the apples, and washes and polishes the biggest one for Michaelmas. It ends with the sentence: *"Thank you," he heard his mother say, "for a beautiful apple on Michael's Day."* Every apple is beautiful. Every apple counts. Every effort is celebrated. The small is elevated to the level of a celebration. I found this story very meaningful for the Michaelmas week.

On the day of Michaelmas we baked a special apple bread. The children helped peel and cut the apples, mixed the dough, and soon the scent of baked apples and cinnamon filled the nursery. The table was decorated with a silk cloth, covered with colorful autumn leaves, as we enjoyed our snack together.

Finally, we went apple-picking ourselves, timed for around the Michaelmas week. This included a walk to the farm, where the old apple trees were laden with apples. All children helped pick them, and we filled many crates for the farmers. On our way home we celebrated the apple picking with a snack of apples.

Doing practical work with the nursery-age children has been one of the most meaningful experiences this year, as we took long walks to harvest potatoes, apples, and rutabagas. In the beginning of the year, I was unsure if the small children would be able to take these long walks, but they were; and not a complaint was heard on those morning outings about fatigue or not wanting to walk. These walks and the work, which can be summed up as repetitive will activities, strengthen the healthy will in the early-childhood-age group, as they do in older children.

The room decoration for the Michaelmas season is easily achieved by hanging felted apples on a simple wreath created of grapevines. In addition, a nature table with autumn- colored cloths and a vase with autumn flowers, especially sunflowers, offers a place for children to bring their treasures into the nursery: another opportunity for them to unite their very being with the space and to celebrate the gifts of nature.

∾

Carol Grieder-Brandenberger holds a Masters degree in Early Childhood Education from Sunbridge College. She taught Waldorf-inspired art classes and parent-child classes before coming to Green Meadow Waldorf School, where she has been a nursery teacher since 2006. Carol enjoys spending time in nature with her two daughters and creating dolls and puppets, and as the Grieder Family Players, she and her husband are known for their traditional Swiss Kasperli puppet shows. Carol is also a Women's Health Nurse Practitioner and pediatric nurse with a background in maternal-child home care.

Michaelmas Story

Bella Schauman

Editor's note: *This story was created for a group of children ages three-and-a-half to four-and-a-half, but it could be appropriate for slightly older children as well.*

The image of the stars showering light at the touch of the stars was inspired by the poem "St. Michael" by I. Tupaj, included in Autumn *(Wynstones Press, 2nd ed.). The image of the lyre was inspired by the story "St. Michael on the Crescent of the Moon," included in this volume.*

One day, just at the end of summer, a little boy went out to the fields and orchards with his father. The air was keen and clear, and the light was golden. The shining sun had filled all the grain so full of summer light that the wheat grains on the stalks were ready to burst from their husks. The apples on the trees were so full of summer sun-fire that they seemed to twist on their stems, eager to fall to the ground.

All day the little boy and his father worked. Father sharpened his sickle again and again. He whistled and sang as he cut the golden wheat. The little boy was supposed to climb high on a ladder to pick the rosy, red apples on the trees. At first he was afraid to climb it. He thought he might fall. But then, he summoned his courage and climbed. He stood high on the ladder in the orchard and filled basket after basket with ripe, rosy apples.

At last it grew late. Father and the boy had worked long and well. They walked home to mother, ate the good supper she had made for them, and went to bed.

That night, while the little boy was sleeping, the Archangel Michael came to him and said, "Come with me. I will show you something special." Michael held the boy's hand, and together they rose higher and higher, until they came to the realm of the stars. The stars shone and sparkled, and as Michael went by he touched each one with his own gleaming sword. Such love and strength flowed from the touch of the sword that the stars showered sparkling light and gleaming trails of fire as he passed.

They went on together, and Michael told the boy how pleased he had been to see him picking apples all day long in the orchard. He had seen the boy standing high on the ladder, filling basket after basket with ripe, rosy apples. Then Michael took his gleaming sword and made it into a lyre. He played on the lyre, and the song he played was so pure and good and true that the little boy listened for a long time.

In the morning when the little boy woke up, he told his father about Michael and the gleaming stars and the lyre music. "I want to see the stars again," he said. His father said, "Come with me. I will show you something special. Today we will not harvest in the fields or the orchards. Today we will work at home."

All morning father and mother and the little boy polished the rosy, red apples the boy had picked the day before. They rubbed and they rubbed, until each apple gleamed. When they had finished, it was time to eat. Mother took a knife and cut open a gleaming red apple. And there, inside, was a star.

෴

Bella Schauman taught a nursery class at Acorn Hill Waldorf Kindergarten and Nursery from 1988-1993. She is now a high school English teacher in Montgomery County, MD.

A Michaelmas Festival for the Parent/Child Group

Cecelia Karpoff and Nancy Foster

Authors' note: *A week before our parent/child Michaelmas Festival, we gave the following brief description to the parents, both to offer some background to this festival, new to many of them, and to help them to participate on the day of the festival. The setting of the center festival table took place during clean-up and bathroom time. The parents helped carry the table in from the hall, spread the white tablecloth (which had been ironed during the morning), and place on the table the festival items described below. One year a colleague was visiting on this day, and her favorite moment occurred when one of the little ones, en route to circle from the bathroom, caught sight of the beautifully-polished apple on the festival table, picked it up, took a big bite out of it, and carefully replaced it—a perfect example of the "bodily religion of the child"!*

⤳

September 29, a few days after the autumnal equinox, brings the festival of Michaelmas, dedicated to the Archangel Michael. (You may hear us pronounce the name in three syllables, which emphasizes the derivation from the Hebrew, Mi cha el: "who is of God.") Michael is known as the conqueror of the powers of darkness, the Angel who hurled the rebellious Lucifer down from heaven. Tradition wisely places this festival day in the fall of the year when we emerge from the more relaxed, even sleepy, pace of summer. School begins, and it seems we all turn more naturally to study and more serious pursuits.

Michael, or his earthly counterpart St. George, battles the dragon, and in this encounter we can see reflected our own personal battle with the "dragon," or all that is base in our lower natures. Michael is connected for us with the will, with our resolve to move forward into the light.

Ancient wisdom portrays two aspects of Michael, as the dragon slayer and as the bearer of the scales of judgment between good and evil. In the classroom we bring the experience of Michaelmas into our work with the wheat, separating the wheat from the chaff, thus mirroring the judgment of good and evil. In polishing apples, we see how the perseverance and diligence we bring to our task results in a bright and shining gift. Both the wheat and the apples are powerful symbols of this time of the year.

The Jewish calendar likewise notes this as a time of new beginnings. There is the celebration of Rosh Hashanah, the New Year; and Yom Kippur is set as a time for reflection and atonement with the weighing of deeds and resolution for the future. Indeed, Michael, by tradition, has a special relationship to the Hebrew People. This is indicated in many tales and legends, and Michael is referred to as "the great Prince who has charge of your people" (Daniel 12:1).

On the day of class following soonest after September 29 we will observe Michaelmas (or Michael's Day) in the classroom. In preparation, we will be threshing and grinding wheat, and washing and polishing apples to be taken home as a special remembrance of the day. The apple slices we have hung on our seasons wreath may also remind of us Michael.

We will set a festival table with a special cloth, flowers and candle, wheat and apples. Snack will be apple crisp. We will sing, "Michael, Michael, with your sword so bright" (see music below), and say this verse:

Michael, Angel bright,
Lead us on with strength and light.

This is how we hope the children will begin to experience Michaelmas, without any necessity for explanations.

Nancy Foster

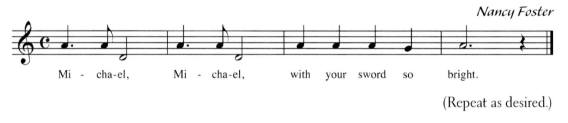

(Repeat as desired.)

Cecelia Karpoff was a Waldorf early childhood teacher in the Washington, D.C., area for many years, including Acorn Hill Waldorf Kindergarten and Nursery, where she developed one of the first Waldorf parent/child programs. The earliest years of childhood and work with parents have been continuing interests and the focus of her talks and workshops, and she is active as a mentor and school visitor.

Nancy Foster was a longtime teacher at Acorn Hill Waldorf Kindergarten and Nursery in Silver Spring, MD, and continues to be active in WECAN and in teacher education. She is author of Let Us Form a Ring, Dancing as We Sing, *and* In a Nutshell.

George and the Apples: A Michaelmas Story for Puppets

Cecelia Karpoff

Author's note: *This table play was created for parent/child groups in which the children were age two to three-and-a-half. Since children of this age do not yet form mental pictures consistently, it is often good to put stories in rhymed verse, so that the rhythm carries the children. It also seems helpful to include explicit "props" to bring the story alive for them. Standing dolls with arms are most suitable for this story of courage. I used the following props:*

- *a sturdy branch for a tree, draped with green gauze or silk, with some red fleece "apples" pinned here and there;*

- *a ladder (mine was made of sticks lashed together with heavy thread)*

- *a small basket with red fleece "apples" and one small red beeswax apple, with a tiny stick for the stem, which George can "polish" at the appropriate time*

- *a small table (piece of wood) in the "house" (a cardboard backdrop draped with silk) where the apple can be placed.*

∽

It works well to sing the song, "Rosy Apples Grow," while uncovering and covering the table.

Once there was George, a little boy.
He played in the garden with great joy,
Jumping like a grasshopper, singing like a bird,
Or watching the butterflies, not saying a word.
He played in the grass and gazed at the sky,
Watching white clouds go sailing by.

There in the garden an apple tree stood,
Full of apples, so rosy and good.
"These apples are juicy," thought George one day;
"I'll pick one to eat, right away."

He reached and he reached, stretched up so high;
He jumped and he jumped; oh, how he did try!
But there on the tree the apples did stay.
For a little boy they were too far away.

Then, "It's Michael's Day," his mother said;
"We'll pick those apples so rosy red."
Father brought the ladder; it reached so high
George thought he could climb to the sky.

(George climbs up the ladder, is made to hold the basket of apples, and climbs back down, while the song is sung:)

Nancy Foster

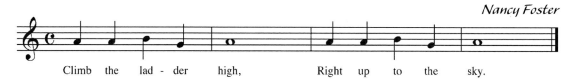

He picked the red apples; then Mother did say,
"Let's make them shiny for Michael's Day."

(George is made to hold and then polish the beeswax apple from the basket.)

George took the biggest and washed it just so,
And he polished and polished to make it glow.

Cecelia Karpoff   *Nancy Foster*

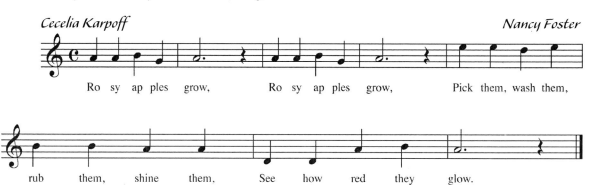

George took the apple with loving care
To the festival table waiting there.

(Repeat song while Father follows George, carrying the basket into the house. Mother goes into the house and they stand around the table while the final lines are spoken:)

60

The table was set; what a beautiful sight;
His apple gleamed like a star so bright!
"Thank you," he heard his mother say,
"For a beautiful apple on Michael's Day."

❦

Cecelia Karpoff was a Waldorf early childhood teacher in the Washington, D.C., area for many years, including Acorn Hill Waldorf Kindergarten and Nursery, where she developed one of the first Waldorf parent/child programs. The earliest years of childhood and work with parents have been continuing interests and the focus of her talks and workshops, and she is active as a mentor and school visitor.

Winter:
Advent, Christmas, and Three Kings Day

Advent:
Preparation for the Adult

Freya Jaffke

Editor's note: *In the following excerpt, translated by Alice Trembour from the book* Feste im Kindergarten und Elternhaus, Teil 1 *(Festivals in the Kindergarten and Home, Vol. 1), Freya Jaffke reminds us how important it is for the teacher to find an inner relationship to the mood of the festival season and offers practical suggestions to support this process.*

*I*n the Christmas Festival a process that has been quietly building for months finds its culmination. As the sunlight wanes, the human soul retreats ever more into itself after having given itself up so happily to the light and warmth of high summer. The balance between light and dark in autumn is like a threshold, and in the darkest time of the year an inner light wants to be kindled. Each year, when Christmas is very close, we make a new effort to bring the outer light in, to transform it so that we are illuminated within and can radiate outward. Others can then sense that tranquility, love, and warmth stream out from such a person as a blessing. Something from Him whose birth we celebrate at Christmas has come to rest in such a person's soul.

Advent means arrival, from the Latin *advenire*, and it signifies that we may attempt yet again to allow something of that high divine being, that connected itself with humanity on earth through the event at Golgotha, to come into us. Each of us may experience how such work on oneself can only be done out of inner tranquility, in quiet moments we have stolen from our everyday lives. And we all know how much more difficult it is to collect oneself, especially in the time right before Christmas, when outer light and a hectic pace prevail. But the children, for whom we create life space and prepare festivals, reward our efforts with their daily joy and inner involvement, and strengthen us in our resolve to see it all through to the end.

One possibility for us as adults to use such stolen moments meaningfully, and allow them to become sources of strength, is to focus on a beautiful verse. If we allow such a verse to be our focus for a few minutes, it can throw its light over the day or week or several weeks, and help us find the right attitude for our work in early childhood education. Through such work perhaps "a light will go on" for us, or something will be illuminated that we did not understand before, or we might begin to glow with enthusiasm. The young child will be able to experience our right attitude through our behavior and gestures, rather than through words. Young children have an unconscious and very fine sense for the thoughts and feelings with which we surround them.

A few examples of appropriate verses appear here; these are but a selected few out of many other verses, and each of us might search out our own.

At the Ringing of the Bells

> To wonder at beauty,
> Stand guard over truth,
> Look up to the noble,
> Decide for the good:
> Leads man on his journey
> To goals for his life,
> To right in his doing,
> To peace in his feeling,
> To light in his thought,
> And teaches him trust
> In the guidance of God,
> In all that there is:
> In the world-wide All,
> In the soul's deep soil.
>
> —Rudolf Steiner, Truth-Wrought Words

Christmas

> The soul's clear eye reflects
> The light of cosmic hope,
> And spirit-devout wisdom
> Speaks in human hearts:
> The Father's eternal love
> Sends forth His son to earth,
> Who sheds, with grace, upon man's path
> The healing light of heaven.
>
> —Rudolf Steiner, Truth-Wrought Words

Light is Love

Light is love ... sun's—weaving
streams of love from a world
of creator beings—
that holds us to its heart
through unending time,
and that finally gave us
its highest spirit in a
human form for three years:
He came as His
Father's inheritance— and became earth's
innermost heavenly fire:
so that it too would one day be of the sun.

—Christian Morgenstern, translation by A.T.

Another way to put oneself in an appropriate mood for Advent and Christmas is to work with the different virtues. If we practice these on a small scale we can even include the children. We must not yet allow the virtue we are practicing to become conscious for them, but we can help them be well-disposed toward good habits through our example, which they will imitate.

Advent is a time of *anticipation*. Waiting is often not easy for us. We want to be finished quickly, and see a result immediately. Waiting teaches us to deal with time. Wishes and fantasies hurry ahead into the future. To fulfill them we need time, and we must wait and overcome impatience. For example, the children experience waiting in connection with the Advent calendar, since they may not open all the doors at once, or with the baking of Christmas cookies, which they may only eat on Christmas or thereafter.

Another virtue is *listening*. Only one who can listen experiences silence, and can endure it, as well. It might be possible to listen with the children in the quiet of a forest, and keep them from making noise, without reflecting on it with them. They especially like to listen to a fairy tale or a story, and all the better if it is told in an intimate atmosphere.

We can direct our *seeing* during Advent especially to the sky, which delights us after a beautiful day with a sunset of strongly glowing colors. The stars shine particularly clearly and close by.

Finally, we can think of *wonder*, which we as adults often must relearn. What a wealth of things there are to wonder at when we sort through our Christmas art postcards, and pay attention to all the various ways the artists here portrayed the adoration of the Child by the shepherds or the kings. In some of the pictures of the "birth," it seems that the mother is in conversation with the Child. And when we create the scene in the stable for the children or our families, we may become aware that we

67

wonder at all the beings of nature that greet the Child as it arrives: stones from the mineral kingdom; moss, hay, and straw from the plant kingdom; sheep, oxen, and asses from the animal kingdom; and alongside them the great distinction of the human form. Wonder is the first step on the way to knowledge/recognition. Wonder also includes respect for certain things. Thus, as we gaze at the stable scene with the children and practice wonder at the events we see depicted there, the children will not take the figures out and use them as playthings.

Each of us may discover and practice other virtues for ourselves. We are not concerned here with quantity, but with helping guide the children through Advent.

෮෯

Freya Jaffke is now retired after many decades of work as a Waldorf kindergarten teacher and teacher trainer in southern Germany. She has lectured and mentored Waldorf kindergarten teachers widely throughout the world. Her books on early childhood have sold over a quarter of a million copies worldwide.

The Turning of the Year: Midwinter and New Birth

Nancy Foster

Author's note: *This article was originally written for the parents of my mixed-age kindergarten class, to share with them our approach to the season of Advent in a way that would allow families of varied religious or non-religious backgrounds to feel welcomed and included.*

⤳

For young children, the seasons and their festivals are experienced as events of nature; with all their senses, the children take in the changes in the world around them. The falling leaves, the frosty mornings, the darkness that falls even before dinner-time, the winter's first snowfall… We can all, if we try, remember the deep responses these sensations awoke in us as children. Along with these perceptions come the children's experiences of human activities through the seasons—now, in late autumn, for example, raking leaves, bringing the houseplants indoors for winter, gathering around the fireplace for a story. It is these perceptions and experiences, and our gratitude for them, that we try to strengthen as we celebrate the festivals together.

As the year draws toward the darkest days of winter, we observe a season of anticipation and preparation for the turning of the year, observed since ancient times, when the sun at the Winter Solstice begins once again to bring longer days. For those who celebrate Christmas, this time is known as Advent. The sense of expectancy, however, can be shared by all, whatever their religious or family traditions, who are sensitive to the deep relationship between the human soul and the cycle of the year's seasons. This time of preparation can be busy, full of hustle and bustle; yet we can also create times of inner calm as we await the coming of new light, and as we experience the love and joy of celebration.

During this season, the children in our class will hear a story of the birth of a child, and the hope, expectation, and joy of this event. Does the telling of this story conflict with the celebration of the festivals in relation to the world of nature? Not at all. As the winter days darken, the human soul longs for new light, for rebirth. The return of the sun at the Winter Solstice is, in a sense, a birth on the cosmic level. On the human level, the birth of a child offers the same experience of hope and joy.

This image of a human birth is full of meaning for a young child; after all, its own birth happened not so long ago and was surely a blessed event in the family. It seems quite right that all the world should rejoice at a birth, and children experience this joy in all innocence. As adults, we may take this in a more sober fashion; we are only too aware that our hopes for a brighter day (i.e. a better world) often seem in vain. Yet this yearly renewal of hope brings us new strength, an opportunity to strive to play our part in fulfilling the hope of this season, looking toward new light. In this way, the observance of the season can speak to the universally human in the child and in the adult, if we can open our hearts to the experience.

☙

Nancy Foster was a longtime teacher at Acorn Hill Waldorf Kindergarten and Nursery in Silver Spring, MD, and continues to be active in WECAN and in teacher education. She is author of Let Us Form a Ring, Dancing as We Sing, *and* In a Nutshell.

Thoughts About an Advent Festival

Stephen Spitalny

Editor's note: *This is the second part of an article, "Festivals," which appeared in the Fall/Winter 2002 issue of* Gateways. *The first part, presenting a look at underlying considerations in creating a festival with young children, is offered in the "Cycle of the Year" section of this publication. We have been unable to find the source of the verse included here.*

As winter approaches in the Northern Hemisphere, there is a growing mood of the outer sleepiness of the world. Through the stories, poems, and songs we bring, and their own observation of nature, the children can experience a settling down, a feeling of being blanketed for a winter's nap. The fallen leaves, the animals in hibernation, the shorter daylight hours which bring us inside much earlier (even in California) than at other times of the year: all contribute to this experience. Advent balances the darkness and sleepiness with expectation and anticipation. It is a time of moving through the darkness toward the yearly rebirth of the light, when the days begin to grow longer. Advent is really a four-week festival, the four weeks leading up to Christmas and Solstice, starting on a Sunday evening. Many religions celebrate festivals of the returning of the light. Among those festivals are Solstice, Chanukah, Christmas, and Diwali. The mood of Advent reminds me of Beethoven's Ninth Symphony—so much preparation for the choral climax that reminds me of the light beginning to grow stronger again.

During Advent, we can deepen our relationship to the world around us through recognizing the strength and beauty in all the four kingdoms of the natural world. The first week is related to the mineral kingdom, the physical foundation for life. The mineral world gives us a fixed stage, a basis for our ever-changing existence. Without the mineral world we would have no ground to stand on.

The second week focuses on the plant kingdom from which we receive nourishment from living forces. Earth, rain, light, and warmth create a balance of growth and decay. The plant world has life that distinguishes it from the mineral world. It is life itself which human beings share with the plants.

The third week focuses on the kingdom of beasts. We share our capacity for movement and feelings with the animal kingdom. In this week of Advent we are reminded of our relationship with the birds, beasts, and other members of the animal kingdom and how they reflect our most basic soul states.

The fourth week of Advent speaks of the human being. All the kingdoms of nature contribute to our existence. We all have mineral, plant, and animal aspects surrounding and supporting the flame of our individual human spirit, this flame that is the essence of what it is to be human. Advent can move us toward a deeper understanding of our place in the universe, of all that supports us and all that we aspire to, as well as all that needs our protection and support.

There are so many levels that one could consider. The weeks can also be connected with the four bodies of the human being, with the four major organs, and so on. In kindergarten, Advent can be celebrated very simply. On the first day, I put one gold star above the nature table on the wall. And each successive day I add another star. Additionally, I set four candles on the nature table. The first week, I light just one of them for a verse at the end of Ring Time. The second week, I light two candles, and so on. The verse I use follows:

The gift of light we thankfully take,
But not alone shall it be for our sake;
The more we give light
The one to the other,
It shines and it spreads and it glows still further,
Until every spark by friends set aflame,
Until every heart with joy to proclaim,
In the depths of our souls a shining sun glows.

I also add something of the particular kingdom of nature addressed to the Advent nature table. Perhaps a crystal or shell is added each day of that week, then the next week, a rosebud each day, then a small wooden animal or feather. There are so many possibilities.

On a Sunday evening in December (determined by various calendar considerations) the kindergarten families come to celebrate the Advent Garden which brings the mood of Advent and the experience of moving from darkness to light to the children in a simple way. This is one festival I set up (with adult helpers) without the children. They arrive to a fully prepared festival space. They walk to the center of the spiral path of evergreens, a path not lighted. One needs to determine which direction the spiral curves, counter- or clock-wise. There are reasons one could have for either. The important thing is to consciously choose the direction. The children bring with them a red apple with a candle that they light from the burning candle in the center of the spiral. They then place their candle carefully down on the path as they walk back out. The festival begins in darkness and ends brightly lit by the many candles. We have a moment to sit in silence together before the children are taken home to bed with their apple candle.

For our celebration, someone enters the dark spiral bearing a candle. He or she is clad in flowing veils, and is not named nor referred to nor spoken about. We try to get someone not generally recognized by the children. It is left to each to imagine what sort of being it is. I invite siblings of the kindergarten children, both younger and older, to participate in our Advent Garden. Younger or less confident children are accompanied by their parents. We have always had this spiral path indoors. This year I have been thinking a lot about doing it in a redwood grove on our school property, under the twinkling stars.

The garden of evergreens is a symbol of life everlasting. Arranged in a spiral, the path represents the path to birth and the process of incarnating. The apple is a picture of the body, the house that we live in. The red symbolizes our blood and our forces of will. The flame of the candle is the flame of our individual human spirit. The Advent Garden is an imaginative experience of our individual spirit light incarnating into life on Earth, and how it is able to dispel the darkness around us. In community, our spirits shining together shed a mighty light.

∾

Stephen Spitalny has been a kindergarten teacher at the Santa Cruz Waldorf School since 1989. Educated in psychology, he met Waldorf education as a parent. He is a former WECAN Board member and served as Gateways *editor for ten years beginning in spring of 2000.*

Choosing a New Name for the Advent Garden

Nancy Foster

Author's note: *This article originally appeared in the December 2002 newsletter of Acorn Hill Waldorf Kindergarten and Nursery. It is included here not to advocate a particular name for the Advent Garden, but rather to share how the name change, as well as the significance of the observance, was conveyed to parents. The faculty had spent a great deal of time and heartfelt thought in deciding to change the name, and in choosing the new name. They felt it was of the greatest importance to share their reasons with the parents, some of whom were eager for a change, while others were quite attached to the traditional name.*

Please note that the history of the Advent Garden given here was drawn from the article by Christof-Andreas Lindenberg included in this volume.

❧

For some years our faculty has been seeking ways to observe the seasonal festivals in a manner which can speak to the universally human qualities in each of us— which can enliven and enhance our experience of the cycle of the year and allow us to celebrate this experience together. Our work, of course, is focused primarily on the needs of the young child; thus, we strive to offer simple, meaningful experiences which can create a sense of wonder, reverence, and joy.

One such experience is the Advent Garden, a tradition shared by Waldorf kindergartens all over the world. After careful consideration, our faculty has chosen a new name for this special occasion, realizing that the name "Advent" can arouse a feeling of exclusion on the part of those who do not celebrate Christmas. It seemed congruent with our search for universality that we choose a new name—one that could include and welcome everyone in our school community. Some other Waldorf schools have also changed the name of this event.

"Midwinter Garden" is the name we have chosen. To introduce this new name and give a sense of its significance, we would like to share a bit of the history of the Garden.

Long ago, we are told, the farmers who lived among the mountains of Bavaria followed a custom at this time of year of bringing in fir-twigs and moss to form a garden on a table, which was then lit up by candles set in apples. For them, this was an expression of an old parable of Paradise; the lighted garden gave promise of Paradise regained.

In 1925 a German nurse brought this custom to Switzerland, to the first curative home for children founded on the basis of Rudolf Steiner's ideas. There the Garden became a yearly celebration held on the first Sunday of Advent. The moss and fir were laid in a spiral path on the floor, leading to the center candle, just as in our Garden. The custom was later taken up by a curative teacher in the first Waldorf School, and it then was passed on to kindergartens in Waldorf schools everywhere.

Taking place at the beginning of Advent, the experience of the Garden reflects the human experience in the world of nature at this time of year: entering a time of darkness, of shorter days and longer nights, and going forward with hope to receive new light at the "rebirth" of the sun after the winter solstice. With the lighting of the small apple-candles, which are placed along the spiral of greens, we can foresee the growing light which will come as days gradually lengthen.

The children's experience of the Garden can also be understood as a recollection of their own birth, which in each case brought a light of its own into the world. In the words of an experienced Waldorf educator, "Deep within the children's souls is stirred a memory of their own spiraling path down to earth, their dream of giving to the earth and all humanity their creative capacities, born of their own inner Light." In the children's faces, we can often see a profound sense of purpose as they follow the spiral path inward, light their candle, and carry it outward to shine in the world, bringing light to us all. It can deepen our experience of the Garden as adults if we reflect that the Garden as we know it was first brought to children in need of special care, who had such special light to bring the world and who had to overcome such obstacles to share it.

Again this year the music of lyres will be heard in the Midwinter Garden. We are most grateful to these musicians for bringing their beautiful tones to accompany the children on their spiral path. It is noteworthy that one of the first uses for the modern lyre, developed in 1926, was at the Advent (Midwinter) Garden. The form of the lyre itself can be seen as a spiral, like the Garden. May the mood of quiet wonder, beauty, and timelessness created by the music pervade the hearts and souls of children and adults who come to take part in our Midwinter Garden.

Nancy Foster was a longtime teacher at Acorn Hill Waldorf Kindergarten and Nursery in Silver Spring, MD, and continues to be active in WECAN and in teacher education. She is author of Let Us Form a Ring, Dancing as We Sing, *and* In a Nutshell.

Stars for the Advent Garden

Susan Silverio

Editor's note: *Here is a reminder of how we can enter into each detail of our festival observances, bringing new life to traditions by considering and deepening the significance of our practices. This article appeared in the Autumn 1996 issue of* Gateways.

*I*n preparing for our Advent Celebration this past season, a question arose about our imagery of the apple, candle, and star. We all agreed that we'd like to dispense with the recycled aluminum pie plates cut into multi-pointed stars which had so ably served as the receptacles for the children's lighted candles since our first Advent Spiral, a family event which preceded the opening of Ashwood Waldorf School ten years ago. We decided to invest in gold metallic mat board available from a framing shop to cut with mat knives into stars, but the question was, "How many points?"

The five-pointed star spoke to us of a certain kind of completion, the image of the upright human being. It was the star which the children know is to be found already within the apple. And yet, with the candle representing the spirit, or the universal, unless it was lighted, would the person be wholly human?

Could it be a six-pointed star? One of our committee reminded us that the six-pointed star, with its two intersecting triangles, could speak to us of the marriage of heaven and earth. We found it appropriate for such a star to be already on the earth when the children entered the garden carrying their apples. The apple bearing the candle, when lighted from the candle in the center of the garden, would be complete, and then placed on one of the six-pointed cardboard stars placed at intervals beside the spiral of greens which compose the garden.

A bit of greenery, tucked around the candle stem, seems to soften this image and bring nature into this picture of body, soul and spirit.

Susan Silverio is the director of the LifeWays Part-Time Early Childhood Training based in Rockport, Maine. She is the lead teacher of Spindlewood Waldorf Kindergarten and LifeWays Center in Lincolnville, and was the founding teacher of Ashwood Waldorf School. Susan is a gardener and a beekeeper.

The Advent Garden and the Lyre:
Something of the History

An Expression of Thanks for the Creators of these Gifts

Christof-Andreas Lindenberg

Editor's note: *In this warm account of the historical background of the Advent Garden, Christof-Andreas Lindenberg offers many details about the individualities and circumstances connected with this much-loved tradition. This article originally appeared in the* Newsletter of the Lyre Association of North America, *Volume 8, Christmas 1986.*

We have always known that it was Dr. Karl Schubert who had something to do with the custom of the Moss Garden on the first Sunday of Advent. If he did not invent it, he must at least have introduced some of the form that makes it. In his remedial class in the Stuttgart Waldorf School he had the children walk and move to various forms, some of which were given to him by Rudolf Steiner in 1922 or 1923. Karl Schubert writes that after a child conference, Rudolf Steiner drew onto paper several forms, amongst them the involuting and outgoing spiral. The child was to move to these forms with his arms and hands, then later to draw these forms himself. To the spiral movements made by the child the teacher is meant to say: "going into" and "going out." Thus, in activating the will, the child works on his rhythmic and sensory systems, involving the whole man, Karl Schubert writes. This was sometime before anthroposophical curative education was inaugurated, and it may well be that such exercises later prompted Schubert to incorporate the double spiral into the layout of the Advent Garden in his classroom. From where did he take the idea of the garden of paradise?

In the German edition of the *Journal for Curative Education and Social Therapy*, Volume 4, 1986, we are told of the history of the custom of this "garden" which in a simplified form came from Bavarian farmers, and was introduced at the Sonnenhof, the original Swiss curative home, by a German nurse working there from 1925 to 1928. Gustel Wetzl knew of the custom of bringing in fir-twigs and moss to form a garden on a table, which was then lit up by candles mounted on apples, an old parable of paradise. In 1925, she shared this custom at the Sonnenhof. The following year on the first Advent Sunday, 1926, this became a formal celebration, with the moss laid out in a spiral path on the floor leading to the middle candle which stood raised on a mount. The candles on the apples were carried there by individual children and after being lit were placed along the path, so that in the end a lit-up garden vouched for paradise regained.

Have the history of the Advent Garden and that of the lyre something in common? Is it not striking that one of the first usages for the lyre was the Advent Garden ceremony! Between the 6th of October, 1926, when the first lyre sounded, and the 28th of November, 1926, the first Advent Sunday, are only a little over 50 days! Could it be a cooperation of muses that these gifts have come to the dark and deaf earth at about the same time, one calling for the other? Light and sound were combining in order to open in a new way the gate to Christmas.

An occurrence from the early years may illustrate this. So powerful was the impact on Dr. Karl König (who later founded the Camphill Villages for handicapped children and adults) when he visited the Advent Garden at the Sonnenhof in 1927 that he then and there decided to dedicate his life to children in need of special care, to the ones who are open to increasing light, to heavenly sounds. Anke Weihs writes: "Dr. König experienced, while watching, an existential human drama: the fateful bite into the apple of the Tree of Knowledge of Good and Evil thrusts mankind into a labyrinth of conflict, isolation, loss of meaning, loss of wholeness. Gently, in the obscurity of special homes, inadequate, sub-normal children would seem to take the bitter taste of that bite away and bring light out of Paradise instead of sin."

Deep in the hardest bone of the head, the temporal bone, lies buried the secret of the cochlea, a spiral structure winding "into" two and a half times, and inside that spiral, the organ of Corti, the most mysterious of organs, allows the act of hearing to come about. One can say that the magic movement of the double spiral with its leap became also the creative movement of the form of the lyre, developed by Lothar Gärtner. Julius Knierim (musician, lyre teacher, and curative educator) never tires of making his students experience the inherent form-principles of the lyre by following them up with one's hand, and what Steiner said to Schubert holds good for that, too: "going into—going out," or "hinein—hinaus." Through such will activity one draws closer to the inscribed secret, as for instance expressed in the constellation of Cancer; in the center you find the nebula Praesepe, Latin for "the manger," into which the child is "born." The sign for Cancer is the double spiral. The Advent spiral harbors more secrets than one! The light-filled sound is born in a new crib! The beginning of all this now is sixty years ago, and for more than half this time I was allowed to be active in the musical part of this birth moment.

Let me describe something personal out of this history. Come with me to the original Stuttgart Waldorf School, after the war, heating in the classrooms being scarce. What encouragement it meant to meet Karl Schubert in the courtyard where he would greet the student with the Austrian "Grüss Gott," your hand getting warmed by his big and warm hand, a shepherd's hand. Once Rudolf Steiner said to Schubert that he carried compassion to wherever he worked! Then travel with me in my memories to Arlesheim in Switzerland to meet and shake hands with the thinker Edmund Pracht. To witness him play the lyre was always an experience of a kingly kind. Pracht once wrote a song for the Advent Garden to words by Karl Schubert, a combination that points to the uniting of the creative elements we spoke of. I never let the Advent Garden ceremony pass without singing and playing that very song, "Holy Mary" (also called "Over Stars is Mary Wandering"), which to me is a perfect example of how the lyre should be companion to the sung melody. There is an elementary character to the "going into—going out," in the interplay between the lyre and melody in this song.

Long since have Karl Schubert and Edmund Pracht entered the realm of true light and sound, yet at certain times one or the other is tangibly present. Being aware of Karl Schubert in this way this Advent time it may be right to have mentioned this double spiral, as I feel he wants us to take this up in a new way. The ever-spreading custom of the Advent Garden is one of the challenges in this direction. So I asked myself how can we introduce a "going into" and "going out" on our lyres, and that especially at that point of the year, the first Advent Sunday, which by tradition is the beginning of the Christian year? New awareness will lead us to answers, and we as lyre players should share what we glean in this search. That in turn will link us to the creative moment in time sixty years ago when the heavens were open enough for impulses of light and of sound to come down to earth, and the gesture of gratitude will be ours in that realization, gratitude to Edmund Pracht, Karl Schubert, Lothar Gärtner and Gustel Wetzl, Johanna Russ, and countless others who brought these gifts to our inner Christmas.

What a different time is it today, how much greater is the need, the need to *go into* the darkness, spreading the light as we *go out*!

༄

Christof-Andreas Lindenberg is a long-time co-worker in the Camphill Movement who has been a musician since his earliest years. He was a co-founder, in 1983, of the Lyre Association of North America, and has brought the music of the lyre into many lives through his teaching, his compositions, and his work in music therapy.

Music for the Advent Garden

Editor's note: *We include the original music for the Advent Garden, by Edmund Pracht and Karl Schubert. The accompaniment is written for the lyre. We are told the song was written in 1927 and published that year in the journal* Die Goldene Leier, *the original dedicated lyre journal in Germany. Apparently several different translations have been made, but it is not clear by whom. This is the version that has always been used in Camphill communities.*

1. Over stars is Mary wandering in her mantle's flowing folds;
Radiant threads of starlight woven for her little child she holds.
Throngs of stars behold her passing, all the sky is filled with light.
With her hands she weaves and gathers blessings for the Christmas night.

2. Asks the sun to weave the sunrays for her cloak so full of light,
Asks the moon to light the pathways for her child and make them bright.
All the stars she fastens, singing, to her chariot row on row,
Wanders through the heavens ringing, comes down to the earth below.
(Verse 1 is repeated.)

—Translator Unknown

1. Über Sterne, über Sonnen leise geht Mariens Schritt,
Lauter Gold und lichte Wonnen nimmt sie für ihr Kindlein mit.
Wenn Maria heilig schreitet von der Sterne Chor geschaut,
Wird von ihrer Hand bereitet, was zur Weihnacht wiedertaut.

2. Ruft die Sonne auf zum Weben für des Kindleins lichtes Kleid,
Bittet dann den Mond zu geben ihrem Kinde Glück und Freud.
Alle Sternlein spannt sie singend an dem grossen Wagen an,
Ziehet durch den Himmel klingend, kommt so auf der Erde an.

—Original German lyrics by Karl Schubert

Over Stars

Voice with lyre accompaniment

Karl Schubert (translator unknown)

Edmund Pracht

O - ver stars is Ma - ry wan - dering; In her man-tle's flow ing

folds, Ra - diant threads of star - light wo - ven For her lit-tle child she holds.

Fine

Throngs of stars be - hold her pass - ing, All the sky is filled with light.

With her hands she weaves and ga - thers Bless-ings for the Christ - mas night.

D.C. al Fine

Building Community
Through the Advent Garden

Joyce Gallardo

Editor's note: *The following is an account of two women's experiences of the Advent garden, one indoors and the other outdoors. They offer a lovely picture of Advent Gardens offered outside a school setting. This article was previously published in* Gateways, Fall/Winter 2005.

The story "Mary's Journey Through the Stars" can be found in The Key of the Kingdom: A Book of Stories and Poems for Children, *collected by Elisabeth Gmeyner and Joyce Russell (Bell Pond Books, 2004, from a book first published by Rudolf Steiner Press, London, 1951).*

An Indoor Garden

On November 6, 2004, my mother crossed the threshold. She would have been eighty-five on November 24. My mother lived a long life of devotion and dedication to her family, as did many women of her generation. During the weeks before Advent, I remembered how Mother had been so touched the first time she attended the Advent Garden and saw my children walk the spiral at the Waldorf school they attended. "How special this is, how beautiful is this garden of light," she commented. Upon awakening one morning, I knew we should make an Advent Garden in our home for the little children who attend Los Amiguitos, the nursery-kindergarten that takes place in my home, and for Mother, to help light the pathway for her.

As I began the preparations, three days before the first Sunday of Advent, I was delighted by the offer of help from my nineteen-year-old daughter, Ana Lucia, who had recently graduated from high school. Now she was ready to give back what had been given to her for so many years, and help to create a magical spiral of evergreens, flowers, and crystals in our dining room for the children and their families who were invited to attend, and for Grandma.

I struggled with the idea of sharing a simple potluck meal after the Garden. Several of the parents had never been to an Advent Garden. Would staying for a meal too drastically change the mood of reverence with which the children would walk the spiral? After each of the Advent Gardens I've attended, children, parents, and siblings would file quietly out of the room and meet their child's teachers at the door outside where they would be handed their apple with the lit candle to take home. Then we would all go to our own homes to have a quiet dinner and lighting of our Advent wreath. The idea was to hold the mood of the spiral that the children had just walked.

But it felt as though something new needed to be created here, a different social impulse, something as sacred as the mood of the Advent Garden with the space in between, the space for meeting the other. I decided that the sharing of a meal and providing the families with a space to meet and commune with each other after the Garden would be important components of this Advent Garden experience.

I asked two parents who are musicians to play Christmas music for us. Vicky led us in singing traditional Christmas carols with guitar, and Juan Basilio, her husband, who is from Nicaragua, played and sang Christmas songs in Spanish. The older sister of one of the kindergarten children, who is a fourth grader, was our Advent angel.

The evening of the Advent Garden flowed beautifully, from the quiet mood of the dark room as I lit the candle and told the story of *Mary's Journey through the Stars*, to the children's mood of reverence as each one placed his apple with lit candle into the spiral, into their joy of receiving their apples with the burning candles outdoors in the cold winter darkness, and then finally into the festive mood of sharing a simple meal together with parents and friends in the light and warmth of the house. A community of twenty-five parents and children ate, talked with each other, played, and sang together on that first Sunday of Advent. Our home was truly blessed by their presence and I could feel Mother smiling.

Benjamin's mother, whose older daughter was the Advent angel, thanked me the next day. "As I watched Benjamin walk the spiral, I knew he was just where he should be. And it was so good to socialize later with each other... it made me realize that we are a community."

Another mother told me later, "It was great to be able to meet and talk with all of the parents. Since I am the last one to pick up my child each day, I have not met several of the parents. This was the perfect opportunity to get to know each other. Thank you for doing this!"

And a third parent, whose son has "graduated" from Los Amiguitos and is now in first grade said, "How important this was for us to come back and reconnect with old friends. It gives us a real sense of continuity, a sense of community."

An Outdoor Garden

A few days later, I shared this experience with my friend and colleague, Susan Weber, and she told me of her experience of the Advent Garden of the past few years.

Susan had had little external festival life since she left kindergarten teaching and felt the need to create something in her home for Advent. The garden behind her home became the space she chose to enliven and use as the place for creating an Advent spiral. She and her husband made a spiral of stones with a candle in the center for the first Sunday of Advent, and they invited their neighbors and the neighbors' young child to come to the garden at dusk. Susan told the story of *Mary's Journey Through the Stars*, they sang songs, and walked the spiral with candlelit lanterns in hand. They placed the lanterns in the spiral of stones and said, "Goodnight."

Susan told me how comforting it was to look out of her window just before going to bed and see the candles still glowing in the stone spiral. This spiral has become a living part of her garden and adorns it year round.

The second week, she and her husband brought evergreen branches to the spiral and celebrated the second Sunday of Advent in the same way, with their neighbors. The third week they brought animals of wood and clay and, the fourth week, apples with candles, one for each child and adult. Each week, the children also hung golden stars in the trees.

Susan told me that they have celebrated Advent in this outdoor garden for the past six years with the same family. The group has grown to four neighborhood families and six children. As the children have grown bigger, they have begun to make the spiral of stones and evergreens and to bring new life to the garden each year as Advent approaches.

Susan emphasized simplicity and continuity as two essential aspects of the beauty of the outdoor garden. The simple representation of the four kingdoms of nature, one for each week of Advent—the mineral kingdom, the plant kingdom, the animal kingdom, and the kingdom of man—creates an atmosphere of growth and life as the time of the Birth of the Light at Christmas draws near. She tells the same story each week of the four Sundays.

"Experiencing the weather each Sunday outdoors, sometimes under a canopy of sparkling stars and bright moonlight, sometimes under a starless sky, and sometimes under flakes of falling snow, has kept us connected to the beauty and power of nature at this special time of the year," Susan added.

Last year, a potluck supper at Susan's neighbor's house was added to their Advent celebration. A space for meeting each other in a new way was created. This festive gathering of children and adults around a big table lit by candles and laden with warm, nourishing food to share on a cold Sunday in Advent helped to keep the light of community alive in the hearts of all who were there, throughout the coming weeks of the darkest time of the year, in anticipation of the Birth of the Light.

The creative potential of Advent (which means *the coming*—the coming of the Christ Child) for building and strengthening community is palpable, "Wherever two or more are gathered together in my name, there am I."

♾

Joyce Gallardo is the director of Los Amiguitos (Little Friends), a N.Y. State-licensed Family Day Care Home, offering a Waldorf Nursery and Kindergarten program. She has taught kindergarten, high school Spanish, and calligraphy at Hawthorne Valley School in Harlemville, N.Y. As the director of Los Amiguitos Puppetry Troupe, Joyce has brought marionette performances to national and international audiences and offered marionette-making workshops to Waldorf teachers in Ecuador.

Susan Weber was among the founding circle of Sophia's Hearth Family Center in Keene, NH, and is currently the Center's director. The Center offers programs arising out of the insights of Waldorf early childhood education, and is enriched by the work of the Pikler Institute.

A Story for the Evergreen Garden

Joan Almon

Author's note: *After fifteen years out of the classroom, I stepped back in as a nursery teacher at the Washington Waldorf School in fall of 2009 to help a friend who was recovering from an illness. As Advent drew near I knew I needed to approach the winter holidays anew. In the past I had drawn heavily on Advent circles learned from European teachers. Now I needed something that spoke to a 21st-century group of American parents and their children and was meaningful to me, as well.*

I thought deeply about the families in my class. Of the thirteen, there were six Jewish families, two Islamic families, one Hindu Sikh family, and the rest I was not sure about. I sought for images that could feed the souls of the children but be accessible to all who walked the spiral of the Evergreen Garden (Washington Waldorf School's name for the traditional Advent Garden).

Over the years I had told many stories about Mother Earth and her creatures, and the changing ways of the forest through the seasons. Now she came strongly to mind. The resulting story also touches on elements of our fall festivals when we cut the apple and revealed the star inside, and when Mother Earth and her creatures observed Halloween and Lantern festivals. The children were used to her by now, and these little three-year-olds listened intently in the darkened Garden.

In the past I did not publish stories or songs until I had used them for several years and they had passed the test of time. I had not thought of sharing this one, but one of the lyre players who was present encouraged me to send it to Gateways where it appeared in the Spring, 2010 issue. I was glad to share it, but please take it lightly and if you wish to use it, feel free to change it as needed. Best of all, let it stimulate your own ideas of how to approach this beautiful Garden which seems to me as relevant today as it did thirty-five years ago when I first created one in my kindergarten.

Winter was beginning. Snow and ice covered the ground and the days were growing dark. Mother Earth called her creatures together and said, "It is time for our Evergreen Garden. It will bring warmth and light to the earth in deep winter. Who will help me?"

"We will help lay a path through the woods," said the stones. "And we shall sparkle in the candlelight like the stars in the sky," said the crystals.

"We shall lay a spiral path of evergreen branches," said the pine and the fir.

"We shall hold the candles," said the apples, "for we have stars in our hearts." The queen of the bees said she would give the wax from her hive to make golden candles.

"I shall bring new life to the garden," said the red, red rose.

The animals of the forest spoke. They would guard the Garden and make sure no harm came to those who walked it.

The stars said they wanted to take part, and some fell to earth to light the pathway of the Garden.

Mother Earth thanked them all and said only one thing was missing—the children's love was needed to fill the Garden.

Then came the children, and one by one they walked the spiral of the Garden, lighting their candles and setting them down on the golden stars. Soon the Garden shone with light.

(Music is played while the teacher walks the spiral, lighting her candle. She is followed by each child and parent, one by one. At the end the co-teacher or assistant lights her candle. The music ends and a closing verse is said.)

Now our Garden is full of light.
It shines with love in the dark winter's night.

☯

Joan Almon is the director of the U.S. branch of the Alliance for Childhood. She is a former Waldorf kindergarten teacher, was co-founder of WECAN, and has worked internationally as a consultant to Waldorf educators and training programs.

Poems for the Midwinter Garden

Nancy Foster and Cecelia Karpoff

Authors' note: *In recent years, those involved in the Waldorf movement have become aware of the need to penetrate to the essence of the festivals we celebrate—to seek, in our observances, a universal aspect which can speak to the hearts of all human beings. Here are the poems we created for use in our Midwinter Garden—Acorn Hill's name for the traditional Advent Garden. They appeared in the Autumn, 1995 issue of* Gateways *and were revised for this publication. The first is intended for mixed-age groups and the second for nursery and parent/child groups.*

Deep Midwinter drawing near,
Darkness in our Garden here—
One small flame yet bravely burns
To show a path which ever turns.

Earth, please bear us as we go,
Seeking Light to send a-glow;
Branches green and moss and fern,
Mark our path to trace each turn.
Brother animals, teach us too
To serve with patience as you do.

We walk with candle toward the Light
While earth awaits with hope so bright;
In the Light which finds new birth
Love may spread o'er all the Earth.

Deep Midwinter drawing near—
May Light arise in our Garden here.

—Nancy Foster

In the deep Midwinter night
There shines a star so golden bright.
Lo, a Child comes down to earth;
Angels greet the happy birth.
All the world begins to sing,
For love and hope the Child will bring.
From heav'n to earth there comes this Light
In the deep Midwinter night.

—Cecelia Karpoff

∽

Nancy Foster was a longtime teacher at Acorn Hill Waldorf Kindergarten and Nursery in Silver Spring, MD, and continues to be active in WECAN and in teacher education. She is author of Let Us Form a Ring, Dancing as We Sing, *and* In a Nutshell.

Cecelia Karpoff was a Waldorf early childhood teacher in the Washington, D.C., area for many years, including Acorn Hill Waldorf Kindergarten and Nursery, where she developed one of the first Waldorf parent/child programs. The earliest years of childhood and work with parents have been continuing interests and the focus of her talks and workshops, and she is active as a mentor and school visitor.

Creating a World Family at Advent Time

Holly Koteen-Soulé

Editor's note: *Here is a picture carried in the mind's eye of one teacher, who found a way to bring it to the children in her group as an experience of a universally human festival observance. This article appeared in the Autumn, 1996 issue of* Gateways.

For the last two years in our kindergarten, the children and I have created a new way to mark the days between Advent and Christmas, which I would like to share with you, my kindergarten colleagues. It began with a desire to re-enliven the journey for the whole class and to honor the diversity of the backgrounds of the children in our kindergarten. The image that kept recurring to me during the fall was of a wreath on which there stood a circle of children representing all the different parts of the world.

While I realized that I could make the figures and dress them appropriately, what I really wanted were authentic dolls made out of a variety of materials and which carried something of the soul quality of the country where they were made. So, on the weekends in November I began scouring the ethnic shops and holiday markets in Seattle. (The most difficult requirement was the size—between two and five inches). My first find was a pair of exquisitely sewn woolen dolls from Bolivia. The girl was carrying a black lamb in her arms and the boy was playing a wooden pipe. After that I looked for pairs of dolls, and they came made of woven straw, carved wood, hand-made paper, cotton, and silk from every continent, including North America.

Every day during Advent, one of the children opened a wooden box in which the new dolls were lying wrapped in a small piece of blue silk. We began with the oldest child. The youngest ones who had watched last year now had their turn to "bring out the dolls." Even in this second year, the mood was incredibly reverent, more so than my experiences with the tissue paper Advent windows (as beautiful as they are). The new dolls sat next to the candle during morning verse. As we walked singing to the table, the opener of the box took the position at the end of the procession, so that he or she had a free hand to carry the dolls. Then the dolls were placed (with a sewing pin or toothpick) on the straw wreath in the middle of the table. The family grew every day until the wreath was full.

This year the first two dolls were handmade paper angels with corn silk hair from India. They "flew" above the wreath on short branches stuck in the straw on either side of the wreath. The Advent candles stood in four star-shaped holders set around the perimeter of the wreath along with a few sprigs of cedar and some tiny alder cones. I watched in particular the responses of the children whose cultures or ethnic backgrounds were represented by the dolls. Although they did not say much, I had the impression that they felt met by this experience. Wonder at the "cosmic child" in every child was certainly there for all of us, as well as a picture which I believe our children also need.

Thank you and blessings on your Advent journey, whatever form it takes.

ര∿

Holly Koteen-Soule was a Waldorf kindergarten teacher for 18 years. She currently teaches parent and child classes and is the Director of Early Childhood Education at Sound Circle Center in Seattle.

The Little Sun Child

Sue Conroy Moran and Cathy Bower

Editor's note: This play originally appeared in Star Weavings, *the Australian Rudolf Steiner Early Childhood Education newsletter. It shows us how a universal aspect of the birth of the light was carried into observing Christmas in the Southern Hemisphere.*

Authors' note: The story of the Sun Child was created in 1991 when we were both teachers/directors of Dawn Song Children's Centre in Bellingen, New South Wales. It grew from our desire to take the familiar story of the birth of light and create for ourselves (and the children) a picture of what is meaningful for us. The Sun Child was performed for our Summer/Christmas Festival as a puppet play, using silk marionettes for the Father, Mother Moon, Golden Glow, and the little Sun Child, and a star puppet for Blazing Bright. We found that the simplicity of the images, plus the repetitive rhythmical quality of the story line, created a stillness within the children as they watched the story unfold. The unveiling and re-veiling of the puppet stage plus the moment of quiet by a lighted taper before the play also aided this mood of quiet.

Long ago and far away, a child lived with his father in a golden castle, high up in the kingdom of the Sun. The Sun Child loved each day to walk in the gardens surrounding the Sun Castle, for there grew the most beautiful flowers, all the colors of the rainbow. It filled his heart with delight, to see them each day, so pretty and bright.

One day, as the Little Sun Child stood looking from his window high up in the Golden Castle, he could see, far, far away, a distant land where no light was shining. This made him sad, for he knew that if no light was shining there, then no flowers could grow to bring joy to the people who lived there.

And so he asked his father, who was very wise, how he could take the light to that distant land, so that flowers could grow there, just like the ones that grew in his garden and brought him so much joy.

And his father replied, "You must travel the path of Starlight, woven bright, and gather as you go, the gifts of shining light." And so the Sun Child bade his father farewell and with joy in his heart, he wove his way upon the starlit path.

Sue Moran

Push the dark of night a-way, so we can en-joy___ the light of day.

He had not gone far when he met Blazing Bright, who was the brightest Star in all the heavens. "Oh Blazing Bright, you shine so bright; have you a gift of shining light? For there is a distant land I know, where no light shines nor flowers grow."

Blazing Bright bowed his head and smiled upon the little Sun Child, "You have a task that is great indeed, take from me this silver seed. Plant it and tend it with love and care, so that flowers may grow there, everywhere."

And so the little Sun Child thanked Blazing Bright and with the silver seed of the stars in his hand he again wove his way upon the starlit path.

Sue Moran

Push the dark of night a-way, so we can en-joy___ the light of day.

Soon he came upon Mother Moon, who was sailing across the heavens, in her full white gown and mantle of silver mist. "Oh Mother Moon, you shine so bright, have you a gift of silver light? For there is a distant land I know, where no light shines nor flowers grow."

Mother Moon bowed her head and smiled upon the little Sun Child. "You have a task that is indeed great, the silver mists of the moon you must take to that distant land below, so that flowers bright may live and grow."

And so the Sun Child thanked Mother Moon and with the silver seed of the stars and the mists of the Moon, and with joy in his heart, he again wove his way upon the starlit path.

Sue Moran

Push the dark of night a-way, so we can en-joy___ the light of day.

Soon the starlit path began to grow dim, and the Sun Child's heart grew sad, for now he could hardly see his way at all. "Oh what shall I do, Oh what shall I do? If I cannot find my way to that distant land below, then the seeds of light I cannot take to help the flowers grow." And he began to weep.

But just then he felt a golden warmth enfold him, and when he looked up, he saw Golden Glow, the Angel fair, the guardian of the Golden Stair. "Oh do not weep, little child of the Sun, I will help you fulfill the task you have begun. Follow me to the Golden Stair; come, I will help to guide you there."

And so, Golden Glow took the Little Sun Child by the hand, and led him to an unknown land, with a sky of blue and clouds of white and a shining stair of golden light. "Here I must leave you on your own, to follow the stair to the land below, and there the seed of light you shall sow, so that flowers bright may live and grow."

So the Sun Child bade farewell to the Angel fair and walked step by step down the Golden Stair. It led him to the land below, where no light did shine, nor flower did grow. Bearing carefully his gifts of shining light, he at last reached the land that was as dark as night. He made a little bed in the cool, dark earth, to hold the seed of light that would bring a flower to birth. Around the silver seed of the stars he wrapped a mantle of Mother Moon's mist, and then in the cool, dark earth he gently laid these heavenly gifts.

"Now, little seed of shining light, you may push away the dark of night, bring a flower to its birth, so that light may live here on this earth."

And so, the little seed began to grow, until at last one day, it did unfold, to bear a flower with a heart of gold. It shone so bright, it filled the dark night with a wondrous, warming radiant light. And from that day to this, many more flowers have grown from that one seed of light that the Sun Child had sown.

The people received each flower with love and gave thanks to the Sun Child who lives high above, for no longer does darkness reign on the earth, now that the light has come to birth.

Sue Moran

The Sun, he is our shin-ing King,_____ Gifts of Light to us he brings,___ King Sun, blaze out with all your might, and push the dark-ness from the light; Push the dark of night a-way so we can en-joy__ the light of day.

Sue Moran first met Steiner Education in Australia as a parent, in 1984. After training and working in Steiner early childhood for seven years, she re-trained as a primary school teacher and has been working as a class teacher since 2002.

Cathy Bower began her path in Steiner teaching as a kindergarten assistant in Australia in 1984. Following her subsequent training at Parsifal College, she taught young children for several years. After some time with her own children, she began class teaching in 1996.

Advent Circle for a Parent–Child Class

Nancy Foster

Author's note: *In a circle for older children or a mixed-age group, transitional material such as a brief rhyme helps to carry the children through the "story line," offering an experience of wholeness that supports dream-consciousness. Circles for a parent/child group are necessarily shorter, and in my experience it is the gesture and movement, and the inner awareness of the teacher, that carry the children, making such transitional material almost unnecessary.*

As early childhood teachers know, the words and music of circles (rhythmic games) are like silk marionettes lying in a storage box. They appear inert, lifeless; we must awaken them to life through the movement and gesture we create for them. It is best when a teacher or caregiver develops meaningful gestures for a circle to meet the ages and needs of a particular group of children, bearing in mind the importance of simplicity and the essential flow of one gesture into another. It would be difficult to do justice to these considerations in attempting to describe possible gestures, so we offer here just the words and music, ready to be brought to life.

In a parent/child group, it is usually expected that the parents imitate the teacher's gestures. The children sometimes simply watch, imitating inwardly, and may not be able to imitate consistently in an outwardly visible way.

This short circle has as its theme the birth of the inner Light that comes in deep Midwinter. The teacher may have the awareness of the following progression through the circle:

- *Preparation (ringing of the bells)*

- *Anticipation (cold, snow, knocking on the door)*

- *Arrival (the Light is glowing)*

- *Offering, serving (cobbler and blacksmith)*

- *Care and nurturing of the Light (cradle song)*

Two additional thoughts entered into the creation of the circle: The original poem "At the Manger" by Margret Meyerkort (from the Winter *volume of the Wynstones Press series) contains four verses, one for each element. I have chosen only earth and fire for this circle, in part because they offer the most vigorous activity—needed in this otherwise very quiet circle—and because they picture the elements brought together in the coming to earth of the Light/Warmth. The closing song, during which we rock the sleeping child in our arms, incorporates what one of our European mentors characterized as the essential gesture of this season, a sort of "rocking into the future." We can experience this as nurturing the potential of what has come to birth—our task as teachers and parents.*

The song "Softly, Softly Through the Darkness" was given to me many years ago by Margret Meyerkort. I do not know the source of the words or tune. A different song with the same words (unattributed) appears in the Winter *volume of the Wynstones series.*

Before the circle begins, the teacher and assistant each put on a bell necklace—a jingle bell on a blue ribbon. On the last day before vacation, each child will receive such a necklace at the end of the morning.

Teacher(s) walk around the inside of the standing circle of parents and children, ringing their bells:

Bronja Zahlingen

Hark, chil-dren, sweet mu-sic, Like of an-gels that sing, Fly-ing high and fly-ing low,—— mak-ing sil - ver—— bells— ring.

(Teachers hang up necklaces and the circle continues:)

Source unknown

Soft-ly, soft-ly through the dark-ness snow is fall - ing, Swift-ly, swift-ly all_____ a - bout, the wind is blow - ing.

O - pen up the door I pray, 'Tis so dark and cold the way.

Clear-ly, clear-ly up_ a bove the bells are call - ing, Bright-ly, bright-ly deep_____ with - in a star is glow - ing.

Hammer, hammer, Cobbler,
Tick-a-tack-a-too.
Lo, the Child will walk the earth,
So work a goodly shoe.

Blow the fire, Blacksmith,
Heat the iron red;
Hammer ploughshares for the Child
To plough the earth for bread.

(Repeat, while sitting down:)

Hammer ploughshares for the Child
To plough the earth for bread.

(Teacher may say: "And now we can all help to rock the Child.")

Nancy Foster

Traditional

While the stars are shin - ing bright, Rock the lit - tle Child of Light,

Sleep-ing soft - ly through the night, We watch the Babe in slum-ber soft-ly dream-ing;

Slum - ber, slum - ber, See the Babe in slum - ber soft - ly dream - ing.

Nancy Foster was a longtime teacher at Acorn Hill Waldorf Kindergarten and Nursery in Silver Spring, MD, and continues to be active in WECAN and in teacher education. She is author of Let Us Form a Ring, Dancing as We Sing, *and* In a Nutshell.

Advent Table Play

Nancy Foster

Author's note: *This table play, which appeared in the Fall/Winter 1998 issue of* Gateways, *is intended for a parent/child or young nursery group. It is easier to perform with two teachers, but it is possible with just one. The words are in part inspired by the song "From Heaven's Arch so High" in the Winter volume of the Wynstones series. The final song is a traditional melody with words created for this play.*

Puppets needed:

* *an angel made of wool roving (white or golden)*

* *two standing dolls as "humble people"*

* *standing dolls for Mother and Father*

* *a baby*

* *a small white bird made of wool batting or roving, with a thread loop to hold when he flies*

The house or stable is a backdrop draped in golden silk under a dark blue silk, with a "bed" of fleece already in place. With the words, "A wonder fills this winter night…" the dark blue is lifted to reveal the golden silk, and the angel can be hung there. At the other end of the tabletop there is a backdrop covered by a cloth over the two humble people, so that it resembles a hill.

The children and parents will already be familiar with the final song, if they have participated in the Advent Circle (included in this volume), so everyone can "rock the baby" and join the singing at a quiet invitation from the teacher.

Nancy Foster

From Heav-en's arch so high,___ A lit - tle Child draws nigh,___

Com - ing soft - ly from a-bove, Borne by an - gels full of Love.

In the darkness of the night
Mother and Father await the Light.
While, awake, the watch they're keeping,
All the earth is soundly sleeping.

Nancy Foster

Now shin - ing ev - er clear - er, The Child comes soft - ly near - er,

In___ the night shin - ing bright, That___ the Earth may take de - light.

A wonder fills this winter night,
With stars aglow in heav'n so bright.
All the heavens are smiling down—
Sun, moon, and stars are weaving a crown.

Nancy Foster

A gent - le bird comes sing - ing, Its hap - py mess - age bring - ing,

"Wake, you peop - le of the Earth, a lit - tle Child has come to birth."

Humble people now awake,
Through the night their journey make.

(Repeat these lines as needed until they reach the baby.)

They stop to hear, stand quite near,
Wond'ring what is happening here.

Nancy Foster   Traditional

While the stars are shin - ing bright, Rock the lit - tle Child of Light,

Sleep-ing soft - ly through the night, We watch the Babe in slum - ber soft - ly dream - ing;

Slum - ber, slum - ber, See the Babe in slum - ber soft - ly dream - ing.

(Repeat the final phrase of the song while covering the table.)

Nancy Foster was a longtime teacher at Acorn Hill Waldorf Kindergarten and Nursery in Silver Spring, MD, and continues to be active in WECAN and in teacher education. She is author of Let Us Form a Ring, Dancing as We Sing, *and* In a Nutshell.

Changing Aspects
of the Winter Season

Nancy Foster

Author's note: *Originally written a number of years ago for the parents in my nursery class, this article told parents of my intentions in presenting the* Three Kings Play for Puppets *(included in this volume) in January. I hoped to convey to them that although the observance of Three Kings Day is a Christian tradition, in a more universal sense it can be experienced as an integral part of the cycle of the year. The "table play" mentioned is the Advent Table Play included in this section.*

When your children return to Acorn Hill in January, they will be seeing a table play of three kings who went on a journey to bring their gifts to a child who had been born in a far-off land. As you know from our observance of the midwinter season, the birth of a child can be seen as a picture of the turning point of the year, as light returns to the earth after the season of growing darkness.

For an understanding of why the story of the three kings is important, following after the midwinter observances, you may wish to consider the following thoughts.

You have heard us use the word "rhythm" many times, in connection with the daily and weekly life of the classroom, as well as with the course of the year and its seasons. Indeed, we as teachers strive to permeate our own as well as the children's lives with rhythm because we feel that this leads to strength and harmony of the whole, healthy individual. The rhythm in the classroom needs to be one that flows freely and naturally, carrying the children comfortably from activity to activity, not one which stops and starts erratically, causing discomfort and fatigue. We might think in terms of a landscape, and seek for hills and valleys rather than peaks and precipices. Even in mountain climbing, the climber hopes to *descend* rather than to fall over a cliff! The gradual descent into the valley allows time for recollections of the ascent and of the experience of the hilltop, and it has its own challenges and delights as well.

Since ancient times the human being has experienced and observed the change of the seasons through festival celebrations. The approach of the winter solstice was one of these times. Long ago, without the modern conveniences of electricity and central heating and automobiles, this time of year must have been a powerful experience in the colder climates: the cold and frozen earth, perhaps deep snows, ever longer periods of darkness. How the people must have hoped and longed for the turning of the year, when even in the continuing cold the days would begin once again to lengthen and they could look with confidence toward the return of spring. Today it is easier to ignore the events of nature, but sensitive individuals can still experience these events, and it seems important for us to arouse ourselves to a renewed harmony with the life of our planet.

When we celebrate the return of the light which comes to the earth, we are aware that it has two aspects: the light of warm-hearted love (pictured in the simple shepherds and their care for the sheep; or the "humble people" of our table play), and the light of wisdom (pictured in the three kings, who were actually wise men of the Zoroastrian faith). According to tradition, the kings reached the child on January 6.

When I began teaching at Acorn Hill, we had not yet learned about the observance of the time of the kings, and I can still remember the feeling of let-down, almost blankness, in returning to school in January—rather like falling over a precipice, actually. Now I can experience how this observance, even in a small, simple way, carries on the rhythm of the year in a smooth and flowing manner. How pleased the children are to see that the newborn child is now visited by the kings! It is clearly a deeply satisfying experience for the children (last year, one child kept asking for the story even in May), yet there is not the intensity of anticipation and preparation— ascending the "hill"— which bears us through the darkest month of the year. Rather, this is a time of quietness, of inner rest, before the stirrings of spring lead us out of the winter "valley."

You may remember that there was a somewhat similar experience of ascending and descending during the autumn. First there were all the preparations leading up to our harvest festival: threshing and grinding wheat, baking, adorning the seasonal wreath, polishing apples. After the festival, we did not fall over a precipice by abruptly turning to other activities. Baking continued, more was added to the wreath, apples continued to be polished, and finally the wreath was transformed by replacing the autumn items with evergreens.

So it is that life in the early childhood classroom flows on. It is our hope that these experiences, brought to the children through activity rather than through explanation or instruction, will form a basis for their future lives. Whatever the philosophy or religion of their families, and whatever path they themselves may choose as adults, it is the experience of rhythmic harmony with the year's seasons and with the events of daily life which will lend them strength both to meet life's challenges and to contribute to the world as free individuals.

Nancy Foster was a longtime teacher at Acorn Hill Waldorf Kindergarten and Nursery in Silver Spring, MD, and continues to be active in WECAN and in teacher education. She is author of Let Us Form a Ring, Dancing as We Sing, *and* In a Nutshell.

The Legend of Babouschka

Adapted by Ruth Ker

Author's note: *From 1995 to 1997, I traveled to Russia several times, visiting different areas of that vast country and offering courses on Waldorf early childhood education. It was a new experience for me to be in a country where the original archetypal stories and the local handwork were still being practiced. Reports from colleagues who are continuing these visits to Russia tell me that this may be quickly changing, so I want to share with you one of the treasures which came my way during my journeys there.*

It is the story of Babouschka, and the setting for the story is imagined by the Russian people I met to be in the northern part of the country. Although I did visit Norilsk, a city north of the Arctic Circle which experiences polar night, forty-five days of total darkness, the translation of this story came from a young university student living in Rostov, a city situated on the Don River near the Sea of Azov. There I met a small group of educators and medical practitioners who were studying anthroposophy in English, French, German, and Russian. These devoted and hardworking individuals were trying to start a Waldorf kindergarten and incorporate some of the Weleda remedies and ideas into their medical practices.

It was telling this story of Babouschka at Epiphany one year in the presence of the intent, shining faces of kindergarten children that gave me a deeper understanding of this story. I have only changed a few words from the original translation. I hope that you also find this story of benefit to your work. Accompanied with a Babouschka circle, there can be a wellspring created for the "kings" in your mixed-age groups. The story first appeared in Gateways *(Fall/Winter 2001).*

Babouschka lived in a little cabin in the coldest corner of a cold and frosty land. Her tiny little house was sitting right in the place where four roads came together. When Father Frost (King Winter) was in the land, then Brother Wind howled at her windows and piles of deep snow piled around her house and hardly anyone ever came to visit her or passed by on those nearby roads. Babouschka's heart yearned for the warmth of summer, the fragrance of the flowers, and the song of the birds, and for her friends.

One year Babouschka decided to prepare a party for her friends. "Then I won't be lonely," she thought. "I will invite all of my friends. I will cook and clean and clear a path to my door through the snow!" Babouschka set to work. She swept her floor and dusted her shelves and washed her whole house. Then she began to cook the most delicious things—her good bread and cookies and cakes—and she also went to her storeroom and brought potatoes and apples and jars of cabbage and tomatoes to her kitchen.

As the day of the party drew closer, Babouschka began to clear the snow away and make a path to her house. When she was outside, she thought she could hear in the far-off distance the tinkling of bells. "Oh dear," she thought, "my guests must be arriving early. I still have much work to do. I'm not ready. I must hurry!" So Babouschka quickly went inside and began to set the table for her party.

She was just putting the plates on the table when the first knock happened. Babouschka went to her door and opened it, but the person standing there was someone she did not know. Babouschka was surprised to see that he was wearing a magnificent crown, and he bent his head to her and said, "Babouschka, we are following a wondrous star in the sky. A special baby is soon to be born. We think He will be a king and that that shining star will lead us to Him. Come with us, Babouschka, and you too can see the newborn king." Babouschka looked past the king and she saw two more kings sitting on camels. She could hear the camel bells ringing as the large beasts stomped their feet. But Babouschka thought of all her friends who were coming, and she said, "I will go with you later, but now I have to get ready for my party." The king sadly turned and left, and Babouschka closed the door behind him.

"Now I must take my bread out of the oven and put the candles on the table," thought Babouschka. That is when the second knock happened. Babouschka once again opened the door and peered into the darkness. She thought she could hear the voices of her friends in the distance, but in front of her out of the darkness appeared another king. His clothes were from a country far away from Babouschka's land, and she thought she could see the light of that star the other king had mentioned shining in his face. Sweet-smelling wisps of smoke floated around the king as he waved a golden censer. He too asked Babouschka to go with him to see the newborn king. Babouschka felt a great stirring in her heart, and she longed to go with the kings, but she looked around her, saw the warm candles of her house, smelled the fresh bread, and said, "I will go another day but I'm too busy preparing for my party now." Babouschka closed the door once again and became very busy sweeping the last bit of her floor.

Then she heard the third knock. "My friends are finally here," she thought. Babouschka ran to the door and threw it open and was surprised to see yet another king. He was young and Babouschka liked him instantly. His smile was a wise one for his young years, and when he too asked Babouschka to come and follow the star, she knew she wanted to go very much. "Stay with me tonight and come to my party," she said. "Then I will go with you tomorrow to see this wonderful king." But the wise king sadly shook his head and said, "We must follow the star. You have many things to offer this newborn king, Babouschka. Bring them with you and come with us too." But Babouschka shook her head. She could see that her friends were arriving. As she welcomed them, her gaze followed the Kings as they mounted their camels and set off on a path toward that great star that filled the whole night with light.

Babouschka had a wonderful party with her friends. They ate the good bread and most of the food, and they danced and they sang.

But when her friends went home the next day, Babouschka thought about those kings and that Baby, and a terrible yearning began to happen. Babouschka quickly gathered up some presents and some of the food left over from her party, and she set out to follow the path of the wise kings. The footprints of the camels were all covered over with snow, but Babouschka trudged onward looking for that great star. She did not find that star or the Baby, so Babouschka gave her presents to a poor family that also had a newborn baby.

Babouschka returned home, but all the rest of that long cold winter and even when the warm time came, Babouschka prepared to go with the Kings when they visited her again the next year.

Babouschka waited for the kings the next winter, but they did not come. So she set out on her own, taking gifts that she had prepared the whole year before. She searched and searched, and again she did not find the Star Child, but she noticed how the children she did find loved the gifts that she brought.

Again Babouschka went home, and she followed the longing that was growing in her heart to find that Child of Light. So it came to pass that with every returning year, Babouschka set out to find that Child the three kings had told her about. Each year, she prepared something for Him, and each year she gave her gifts to children who smiled and delighted in her presents. Babouschka grew to love the children greatly.

One Christmas, Babouschka had hardly anything left in her house to give. She was old now and had given much to many children and their parents. She had found an old toy and was busy polishing it when she heard a soft cry outside her door. "That sounds like a baby," she thought. "Who would leave a child outside on a cold night like this?"

Babouschka quickly went to her door and opened it. She looked out into the cold dark night and there, on her doorstep, she saw a basket. In it was a shining baby, and when he saw the polished toy in Babouschka's hands, he held up his little hands and cooed with delight. Babouschka's heart filled with joy. Then she looked up and saw that there, standing near the Child, was an adoring mother and father, and behind them were the three kings who had come to her door on that night long ago, and around them were all the children and parents whose hearts Babouschka had lightened. They had all come to Babouschka's hearth... and then, Babouschka knew that nothing had been wasted. She knew that all of her efforts to find the Child of Light had been worthwhile. Her heart was full of love.

❀

Ruth Ker is a kindergarten teacher at the Sunrise Waldorf School on Vancouver Island in British Columbia and is currently a member of the Board of WECAN. She is active in research locally and internationally for the benefit of the older child in the kindergarten and edited the WECAN book You're Not the Boss of Me! Understanding the Six/Seven-Year-Old Transformation.

Three Kings Puppet Play
for a Parent/Child Group

Cecelia Karpoff

Author's note: *This simple play requires puppets for Mother, Father, Child, and the three Kings. Our Kings were in the primary colors—one possibility; the more traditional colors of red, blue, and green could be substituted. The dialogue of the Kings and Mother and Father is derived from a circle play handed down to us in the 1970s, originally compiled by Johanna-Veronika Picht, who taught at the Stuttgart Waldorf Kindergarten Training Seminar for many years. The song by Julius Knierim was included in that play, and I do not know its original source. I am most grateful for these materials.*

Sing while uncovering the table:

Gold-en, gold-en shines the star, shines the star so bright - ly; Gold-en, gold-en

shines the star, shines the ___ star so bright - ly.

Away in the East a golden star
Called three wise Kings from afar;
It shone so brightly in darkest night
And beckoned them on to the Child of Light.

J. Knierem

Wan-der-, wan-der on and on, winds and clouds are com-ing a-long;

Wan-der sun and moon and star, Till we find the King a-far.

The Kings came riding, one, two, three,
Over the desert, over the sea,
They followed the star to the Child so bright
And offered their gifts to this King of Light.

Yellow King:

Oh dearest Child, I bring you gold;
For you its glory shall unfold.

Red King:

With all my heart I bring with me
Frankincense to honor Thee.

Blue King:

Myrrh is what I offer You;
Take my love and praises too.

Mother and Father:

Thank you for the gifts you bring;
Thank you, oh royal earthly Kings.

J. Knierem

Wan- der -, wan - der   on   and   on,   winds   and   clouds   are   com - ing   a-long;

Wan - der   sun   and   moon   and   star, ___   Yes,   we   have   found   the   King   a - far.

(Sing "Golden, golden…" while covering table.)

Cecelia Karpoff was a Waldorf early childhood teacher in the Washington, D.C., area for many years, including Acorn Hill Waldorf Kindergarten and Nursery, where she developed one of the first Waldorf parent/child programs. The earliest years of childhood and work with parents have been continuing interests and the focus of her talks and workshops, and she is active as a mentor and school visitor.

Spring/Summer: Easter and Whitsun

Spring Awakening

Freya Jaffke
translated by Eva Gardner, revised by Lory Widmer

Editor's note: *In this excerpt from her book* Feste im Kindergarten und Elternhaus, Teil II (Festivals in the Kindergarten and Home, Vol. 2), *Freya Jaffke describes life in the kindergarten during the time leading up to the Spring/Easter festival. She also offers thoughts about the inner preparation of the adult in seeking a deeper relationship to this festival season.*

When winter—with its cold, its darkness, its strong form structures revealing themselves right into the crystal-clear formations of the snowflake—slowly recedes and spring announces itself, then nature begins to rise and flow again. The light increases distinctly and early warmth approaches; new life awakens everywhere and breaks forth. Buds are swelling on trees and shrubs; the first snowdrops, winter aconite, coltsfoot, and crocuses open toward the light of the sun. The air is filled with gentle fragrances, the animals awaken out of their winter sleep, flocks of birds return and are heard in manifold twitterings. The children too press more and more toward the outdoors and daily discover and welcome something new.

When the time appears ripe, depending on the weather, we now uncover the garden beds where the tulips and narcissi stretch out their first green leaf tips. Ever and again comes our song about "Mother Earth, Mother Earth, where are your little flowers? Sleeping, sleeping within the earth, until awakened by the sunshine," which we sing and play in the spring circle. A little rhymed story about "Drake, the Dwarf" (*Zwack, der Zwerg*) enjoys a particular popularity and supports the spring mood as well.

Drake, the Dwarf, buried a bulb
Deep in the woods where he did dwell,
And soon, when Spring was coming close,
A little flower was seen to swell.

Drake the Dwarf called, "Mr. Hare!
Hop out of your hollow home,
Run and tell to all the tidings
That my little flower did bloom!"

So the larks from high aloft,
And the moles from moss so deep,
And the fawns from farthest forests,
As fast as they could fly or leap,

All drew near—Oh see here!
Bend your heads and bow your gaze,
See the blossom that blooms to bring us
Tidings of Spring's blessed days.

—*Author unknown, translated by Lory Widmer*

For children in large cities a spring awakening may also be experienced in nature if they are taken for regular walks in the parks and are allowed to remain for a time with everything they discover. Every glittering stone; the ants which are industriously carrying their eggs away; the many maple seedlings which are suddenly unfolding—everything delights the childish heart when an active adult sympathy and love for nature surrounds it. And when observing a snail slowly creeping along, they immediately think of the snail verse.

Oh how slowly, oh how slowly
Goes the snail upon his track!
Seven endless days it takes him
Just to crawl one way and back!

Oh how slowly, oh how slowly
Creeps the snail through the grass!
If I would be such a creature
I would not so slowly pass!

—*F. Gull, translated by Lory Widmer*

Something of this spring mood can also be brought into the home in that we decorate the seasonal table appropriately. It has a green mat that is partly covered over by a light pink veil. A large vase with budding branches and small vases with early spring flowers have been placed on it. Also, the many things collected by the children, such as empty snail houses, can find a place here. In anticipation of Easter a basket has been prepared in which blown-out eggs are collected.

In the ten days to two weeks before Easter we have a big spring cleaning time. After the long winter and in anticipation of the impending festival, this cleaning, refreshing, renewing effort is a stimulating activity in which the children will participate joyfully. If the spring days are warm, much can also take place outdoors; notice the fresh aroma that the laundry now has, drying in the spring air!

In some kindergartens, before the beginning of the Easter vacation, the children may also paint a blown-out egg. These eggs are placed into a basket and covered for Easter. Thus the children see a little of what is planned, but at the same time learn that it is important to wait for the right moment. Later, when the children return from the holidays, these eggs will hang in the Easter bouquet.

The preparation of the adult

After the spring equinox on March 21 the sun precedes the moon victoriously; its daily arcs expand and grow ever higher. Thus, as the days begin to lengthen, on the first Sunday following the spring full moon, we celebrate the Easter festival.

The actual Easter theme is "death and resurrection." A deeper understanding needs to ripen gradually within the child's soul. It is constantly surrounded by death and growth processes, and during the school years these begin to light up in the thinking consciousness.

As nature teaches in many ways, the germ for new life is already contained within every death. After buds have already been formed in the fall in order to provide for new leaves, the old leaves are dropped and the life forces withdraw. Ripe fruits may provide nourishment, or they may also die off and rot. In them new seeds are formed, where as soon as suitable conditions are ripe for it, the new plant breaks forth. In the animal kingdom the caterpillar reminds us of this when it flies forth out of the dark pupal stage as the transformed butterfly. Already in the old mysteries this natural phenomenon was a symbol for the immortality of the soul, and Goethe's *Faust* ends with the words: "All that is transitory is but a symbol."

The mighty transformation that occurred on Golgotha two thousand years ago is not easily accessible for today's humanity. We must start on the path quite consciously if we wish to really absorb the Mystery of the resurrected divinity. The modern spiritual knowledge appropriate to human consciousness in our time, which Rudolf Steiner has transmitted to us, can be of help. In many of his lectures on the annual festivals the Mystery of Golgotha is also a central thought. If we open our soul for such mighty events and try to deepen our thoughts from year to year, we shall acquire a much more intensive relationship to our activities with the children at Eastertime, as well as with all other Christian festivals. For the small children, who are still connected with everything through their sense experiences, it is most important for us to reveal our thoughts in deeds and gestures and guide them in a living way into natural phenomena without explanations. This will be a good foundation through which, in later years, they will gradually be able to grasp and understand the greatest secrets and connections in spiritual realms.

Preparation for the Easter festival; the Easter garden

One of the most suitable and striking images for the transformation of death and resurrection is that of the seed of grain. Thus it is a wonderful and significant activity to sow seeds with the children in the time before Easter. For the educators' preparation, it is important that on the previous evening they occupy themselves inwardly with the special moment of sowing, so that on the following day they may be effective in the right way through their gestures. For a deeper experience to arise, in the above-mentioned sense, everything depends on the attitude with which we suffuse the joyous and busy activities.

The time of sowing depends somewhat on the choice of seed. Summer wheat grows two to three inches (five to seven cm) high within a week. Grass takes somewhat longer, but no more than two weeks. It also depends on the location of the garden, humidity, and temperature.

To begin with we fetch earth out of the garden, which we crumble very fine, separating out all stones and little branches. When we find an earthworm, small beetle, or centipede, then we return it to the garden bed. A part of the earth we sift into a second pot. This work can easily be done outside if it is a sunny spring day, otherwise in the room at specially-covered tables.

On the next day we fill the clay bowls which the children have brought, first with the crumbled earth, and on top adding a layer of the sifted earth, which we pat gently by hand. Now the teacher starts the sowing, and the children watch. And ever again the words ring out:

We're sowing the seeds, the seeds so small,
Over the earth we sprinkle them all.
We cover them up,
To rest in sleep.

Soon green sprouts are showing
Some little plants growing,
They peep through a chink —
We'll give them a drink.

And if we're patient, then we know
Our Easter grass will surely grow.

—*Author unknown, translated by Lory Widmer*

Or else, the song will resound: "Swish, swish, the sower is sowing...."

To begin with, some children—perhaps the more dreamy ones—will lay their seeds into the center. Others are not satisfied until the whole surface has been covered and no earth is visible any longer. The teacher stands by, helping them. We cover the seeds with a very thin layer of fine earth and "now they rest in place," as we have learned from our rhythmic games.

Just before we place the little gardens on the window sill, we let it "rain," watering them gently with the laundry sprinkler. During free play time we are completely occupied with filling the clay pots and sowing. Everyone is able to attend quietly to his or her own activity. Some children are always gathered around the teacher while others continue playing. If the gardens are kept moist daily, the first green tips will already show themselves after three to five days; these of course will be greeted joyfully by the children and virtually pulled out of the earth with their gaze.

On the last day in the kindergarten, before the Easter holidays, the children will take their gardens home in order to place them, on the evening before the holiday, in the garden, the balcony, or indoors, ready for the Easter rabbit.

After Easter it is important that the small gardens are returned to nature and do not end up in the garbage pail. Thus we plant them at the meadow edge, in the garden or park.

In this time also, while in the garden or on their walks, the children love to make small Easter nests for themselves out of moss or pine needles, into which they place stones, snail houses, pinecones and other things.

℅

Freya Jaffke is now retired after many decades of work as a Waldorf kindergarten teacher and teacher trainer in southern Germany. She has lectured and mentored Waldorf kindergarten teachers widely throughout the world. Her books on early childhood have sold over a quarter of a million copies worldwide.

Seeking the Essence of the Festivals: Easter and Whitsun in the Kindergarten

Barbara Klocek

Editor's note: *This article places Easter and Whitsun in the context of the year's festivals, illustrating that these observances are part of a living whole. It also exemplifies a teacher's striving to penetrate the deep significance of each season as a necessity for bringing joy and meaning into the festival life of the kindergarten.*

⤸

*E*arly childhood teachers recognize that one of our tasks is to bring the young child into a wonder-filled, yet truthful, relationship to the world. As the children greet each day with eager anticipation, we are there to welcome them to the rhythms of the day, the week, and the year through circle time, activities, and story. How do we form a curriculum that brings them living experiences of the seasons and the festivals?

As a Waldorf teacher of many years, I have come to feel that the seasons and the festivals are our curriculum. In seeking to deepen my work, I have sought guidance from anthroposophical sources as well as from nature herself. I have found renewal and enthusiasm in studying the indications of Rudolf Steiner concerning the festivals and their deeper aspects in relation to the evolving human being. *The Calendar of the Soul* by Rudolf Steiner has provided insight into the breathing of the human soul with the World Soul. In addition to a daily reading of the verse for the week, I have found Karl König's *Rudolf Steiner's Calendar of the Soul—A Commentary* invaluable. It was here I was led to understand that the festivals from Christmas to Whitsun are the festivals that are "given" from the spiritual world. From Whitsun to Christmas, the human being makes the journey of finding the way back to (or carrying gifts back to) the spiritual world.

What then are the mysteries that stand behind these festival times? What are the great archetypes and processes that are mirrored in these festivals? Which are universally human, which are culturally based? Certainly the great portals of birth and death stand before each human being as a mystery. These two have their outer expression in my particular culture (as an American in California) as Christmas and Easter. We may bemoan the "materialization" that modern culture has created around these festivals, but it is our calling, as teachers of young children, to find and bring to them what is good, beautiful, and true in the mysteries behind the festivals.

Seeking to bring these thoughts into my daily experience, I work with the Christmas picture as one of birth. Depending on the culture of an individual school, this picture can take many forms, from the birth of light in the darkness to the birth of the Child. I have for many years told the story of Mary, Joseph, and the Child as a fairy tale, loosely based on the Oberufer Shepherds Play. This has resonated wonderfully with the children in my class and created a lovely echo in the birthday story they hear for their own birthday. My goal has been to give them in picture form the essence of the journey to birth. We often sing some traditional carols within the story to give them a context for these songs. Of course in other schools this may not be appropriate or even possible, in which case the teacher will find other ways to bring the imagination of this season.

Easter presents a different question. Its meaning is more elusive; even as adults we must continually seek for new understanding concerning death and resurrection in the Easter imagination. We seek and find different understandings of what this season brings (for example, why death in spring?). This search is reflected in the tradition of the hiding and finding of eggs.

Rudolf Steiner has been a source of much of my inspiration, giving many insights which can bring meaning to our work with children. I have sought to bring images from nature, of life springing out of apparent stillness (death), as well as transformation. This has included bringing in frog eggs, waiting and waiting and watching for them to hatch and turn slowly into tadpoles and then frogs. I also bring in silkworms which lie still and quiet for several weeks as eggs. These have been stored in my refrigerator and when they hatch are the size of an eyelash. As soon as they eat and eat the mulberry leaves, they turn green and as large as your finger. Thanks to our warm weather here, the children are able to watch them spin the silk into cocoons and once again seem to die (or become very still) until they hatch as moths. After a few weeks of laying their eggs, the moths will die as well, leaving us once more with the very still and quiet eggs within which lies new life.

Then there is the abundance of nature around us in spring. Flowers begin to bloom, leaves come out, and baby animals are born. A symbol of all this plentitude is the rabbit, which is very prolific in reproducing. While the European tradition speaks of the Easter hare, I have found that the children in our area (where there are no hares) have no relationship to them. So instead, I try to re-envision rabbits. Four weeks before Easter, we begin making collars for our rabbits by twizzling two colors of yarn together. Name tags will be attached to this collar, with the child's name on one side and the rabbit's name (which the children give) on the other. Then it is time to make our rabbits. They are wet-felted by the children over the next week or so. I have both white and dark roving, and they choose what combination they want. I make one loose knot for the body and another smaller one for the head, with the end of the roving divided to make rabbit ears. I wrap another layer of roving around it to cover the knots. Then I dip it into warm water and lavish it with good-quality dish soap. Gently the children squeeze and then rub their rabbit for five or more minutes. I encourage them to keep the rabbit plump so it does not become skinny. They then rinse the rabbits in warm and then cool water. While the children dry their hands, I squeeze a little more soap out of the rabbits (some remaining doesn't seem to matter). Then I ask each child if it is a sitting-up rabbit or a lying-down rabbit and shape it appropriately. I tell them the eyes will be open tomorrow.

I take the rabbits home that night and do only a *little* needle-felting on them and add eyes. The eyes are simply a thick yarn through the head, which is needle-felted to stay in place. The children love their rabbits, making houses, boats, and so on, for them and involving nearly everyone in their play. As Easter draws near, we plant wheat grass, make Easter baskets from a painting, and sometimes do more wet-felting of eggs, seed babies, pouches, or other springtime forms.

Circle time has enriched the experience as we become farmers who plant our wheat, with verses and songs about butterflies and moths emerging and the Easter rabbit who paints eggs with the blue of the sky, the yellow of the sun, and the red from the strawberries. We have the children bring in blown eggs and we also purchase and hard-boil many for our Easter egg hunt the last day before our spring break. At our regular painting time, we dye our eggs with Mercurius tissue paper. Several parents have hidden the eggs on Friday morning before spring break. At recess the younger children first find two eggs each, then the older ones. All the eggs go into a common basket (from which the teachers sometimes quietly hide more eggs). Soon groups are hiding them for each other and the recess goes quickly. That day the Easter baskets go home and we all are left with the feeling of abundance and mystery.

Whitsun celebrates the time when the Holy Spirit descended upon the disciples, filling them with the Spirit so they were able to speak in every language of the people. It is the festival of the brotherhood of all human beings. For my class, I bring images of birds in circle time, as the Holy Spirit is often depicted as a white dove. In the circle the white bird calls down to the people to see one another as brothers and sisters:

In the heart of everyone shines a sun so bright.
Listen to the song in the heart of everyone.
With the Sun as our Father and the Earth as our Mother,
Brothers and sisters we are to each other.

We then do the game of "Bluebird, bluebird through my window," but I have changed the words to:

White bird, white bird, through my window,
White bird, white bird, through my window,
White bird, white bird, through my window,
Singing out with joy.

Then, beginning as the teacher, I stand behind a child and sing:

Find a dear friend and touch him on the shoulder,
Find a dear friend and touch him on the shoulder,
Find a dear friend and touch him on the shoulder,
Singing out with joy.

As the children are touched, they join the teacher, and soon everyone is included.

Seeking the essence of these festivals, we find they nourish both the children and ourselves. These festivals are gifts from the spiritual world, of birth at Christmas, death overcome at Easter, and finding our oneness as a community at Whitsun. Through them we are given the inspiration to carry the light we have been given into the darkness of the second half of the year, when we are accompanied by the Archangel Michael.

ᘒᘒ

Barbara Klocek has been a kindergarten teacher at the Sacramento Waldorf School for many years. She holds an M.F.A. in fine arts and has worked as an art therapist. She has raised three sons and loves music, nature, and art. With her husband, she tends a bountiful garden.

Searching for the Secret of Rebirth and Renewal

Holly Koteen-Soulé

Editor's note: *Here we read of a teacher's discovery that the archetypal meaning of the Easter/spring season is congruent with the evolving capacities and needs of the older children in her kindergarten, and how this congruence results in a joyful festival observance.*

*I*n Rudolf Steiner's lectures, *The Four Seasons and the Archangels,* he describes the different qualities of each season with its respective archangel and explains how the changing relation between the earth and the cosmos affects human beings during the course of the year.

He tells us that during the winter, cosmic spiritual forces descend like a graceful mantle of snow upon the being of the earth and its inhabitants, in a kind of calm benediction. In the spring, however, myriad forces are awakened and become active in the chaos of new growth. The weather, too, is mercurial, and most of us can relate to that heightened sense of longing often referred to as "spring fever."

Finding a healthy balance between our earthly and cosmic natures is the task of the spring season, and Steiner offers us for inspiration the archetype of the "Representative of Humanity" standing between Lucifer and Ahriman, keeping them in their rightful places. Raphael is the guiding spiritual being of the season and also stands for the healing impulse in nature.

Other guiding thoughts appear in Steiner's *Calendar of the Soul.* There we begin to understand that spirit beings become "enchanted," as it were, into the renewing plant world in spring. We see that in springtime, the human soul is also drawn out into nature through the senses, but that memory and thinking must be called upon to help keep ourselves in balance. Thus we must be inwardly active rather than succumb to dreaminess.

In pondering the cosmic qualities of the spring season, I asked myself how I might work with these profound realities and weave them into an appropriate experience for the young child. The nature of early childhood makes clear, first of all, that the mood of the experience must be active rather than passive. I also wanted to take into account that the first-grade-ready children in my mixed-age kindergarten class were seeking new challenges for their ripening forces. The result of all these musings was a treasure hunt I created as an integral part of our Spring Festival.

The "treasure" for our hunt was different from year to year—chicks, eggs, nests, or rabbits—one for each child, wrapped together in a cloth and placed in a basket. While the children treasured their gifts, the real prize (just as in the traditional Easter egg hunt) was in the activity, in finding what they were looking for!

The treasure was to be found by following several clues, each of which was a familiar nursery rhyme. The rhymes were written on cards in colored pencil, each with a simple crayon illustration accompanying the verse. The first nursery rhyme led the children to a place in the nearby park where our hunt took place. This rhyme revealed where the second clue was hidden, and so on.

Of course, I read the nursery rhymes for the children. The listening was intense and filled with dramatic anticipation. Sometimes a guess was shouted out and at other times, the whole group just ran off together in a common direction, thinking with their feet! I had a large group and usually did this activity only with the older children. However, with a smaller group, the younger children would undoubtedly follow along with equal enthusiasm.

For example, the first clue might be "Jack and Jill went up the hill." The key word might be water and the second clue would be hidden near the outdoor water faucet.

Other nursery rhymes that could be used include:

"Mary, Mary, quite contrary" (flower garden)

"Daffodowndilly has come to town" (daffodil patch)

"Goosey, goosey, gander, whither dost thou wander?" (stairs)

"Hickety-pickety, my black hen" (chicken coop)

"Rock-a-bye baby in the tree top" (tree)

"The grand old Duke of York" (hill)

"There was an old woman who lived in a shoe" (cubby room)

The children were challenged to connect the pictures they saw inwardly while hearing the nursery rhymes to familiar places in their environment. You can imagine their delight when their intuitions were confirmed.

The treasure hunt evolved as much out of my observation of the growing capacities in the children as my study of the cycle of the year. However, when I reflected on our festival year, I realized that our autumn celebrations nourished predominantly the children's will and our winter festivals, their feeling life. It made sense that our spring festival should activate their thinking.

The treasure hunt is also an archetype of the search for something of value that is hidden from ordinary sight. At Easter time, that signifies to me the renewing force of spirit that lies behind the burgeoning growth of the plant world, of the Christ Being working in the etheric realm of the earth.

We must use all of our soul forces to bring balance and healing to our souls and to the world, but in spring, Rudolf Steiner reminds us, it is our enlivened thinking that allows us to lose ourselves in the beauty of the season, and by doing so, to find ourselves.

௸

Holly Koteen-Soulé was a Waldorf kindergarten teacher for eighteen years. She currently teaches parent and child classes and is the Director of Early Childhood Education at Sound Circle Center in Seattle.

Lady Spring Visits the Kindergarten

Marjorie Thatcher

Editor's note: *Here is a description of a Spring Festival which, though quite simple, clearly evokes a sense of wonder in the children as they enter a beautifully-prepared environment and experience the coming of spring.*

〜

*T*he children sit on low benches in a semi-circle in the eurythmy room, each clutching a peat pot filled with potting soil. The center of the room is decorated with pastel silk cloths and vases of flowering branches—forsythia, cherry, flowering plum—with pots of vibrant primroses beneath them. There is an expectant silence. One little boy next to me whispers, "Does Lady Spring wear all those shoes?" He is gazing at the open shelves where the eurythmy shoes for the grade school children are stored.

There is a gentle tap on the door. It is opened and Lady Spring is welcomed in. She is dressed in a green gown (borrowed from the eurythmy teacher) and wears a crown of spring flowers—primroses, when possible. Lady Spring is usually a twelfth-grade student not known to the children.

Lady Spring is greeted with the song "My Lady Spring is Dressed in Green" from the *Spring* volume of the Wynstones Press series. She walks slowly around the room, placing two seeds, usually sunflower seeds, from a basket into each child's peat pot. Carefully, she presses the seeds into the soil. The children continue to sing the spring songs they have been learning. "The little raindrops patter upon the earth today" is a familiar one in Vancouver.

With another song, "Mother Earth, Mother Earth, take our seed and give it birth" from Elisabeth Lebret's *Pentatonic Songs*, Lady Spring takes a small watering can and gives each peat pot a little water. When the watering is completed, she waves goodbye and leaves the room. Carefully, the pots, each labeled with the child's name, are collected in a basket, and we all return to our classroom to continue the morning routine, with a special snack and story.

We care for the seeds in the kindergarten until the seedlings are several inches tall and then they go home.

୭୬

Marjorie Thatcher taught kindergarten, preschool, and parent/child classes at the Vancouver Waldorf School for twenty-nine years. She is a co-founder and co-director of the Waldorf Early Childhood Training offered by the West Coast Institiute for Studies in Anthroposophy in British Columbia, in which she teaches classes on the festivals. She is very grateful for the rich experience of festivals in her childhood.

A Story of the Easter Hare

Editor's note: *This story appeared in* An Overview of the Waldorf Kindergarten, Vol. I (WECAN, *1993). It was prefaced by this explanation:"The following story was told by Johanna-Veronika Picht, who taught at the Stuttgart Waldorf Kindergarten Training Seminar for many years. It is based on a tale told by K.E. Proske. The origins of the tale are not known. We have seen other versions of this story, as well, in which the order of the eggs is different. Teachers can feel free to adapt the story. In translating it, the German word Hase has been translated as 'hare,' even though in North America we speak of the Easter rabbit, not the Easter hare. But the hare is a different creature from the rabbit and is more intimately linked with Easter and its great story of sacrifice, for the hare is willing to sacrifice itself in order to save other hares."*

*O*nce there was a father Easter hare and a mother Easter hare, who had seven children, and they did not know which of them was to become the Easter hare. Then the mother Easter hare took a basket with seven eggs, and the father Easter hare called the seven children and spoke to the eldest. "Take an egg out of the basket and carry it to the garden by the house where the many children live." The oldest hare took the golden egg, carried it through the wood and over the stream, came out of the forest, hopped across the meadow, and came to the garden of the house. There he wanted to jump over the gate, made one leap which was much too large and mighty, and the egg fell and broke. He was not the true Easter hare.

Now the second one had his turn. He took the silver egg, carried it through the wood and over the stream, came out of the forest, and hopped across the meadow. There the magpie called, "Give the egg to me, give the egg to me, and I'll give you a coin." Before the hare saw what was happening, the magpie had taken the silver egg into her nest. He was also not the true Easter hare.

Now it was the third one's turn. This one took the chocolate egg, carried it through the wood and over the stream, and came out of the forest. Just then the squirrel came running down from the tall fir tree, opened his eyes wide and asked, "Does it taste good?" "I don't know, I want to bring it to the children!" "Oh, just let me taste it!" The squirrel licked it and because it tasted so good, the rabbit licked and tasted it with him—until the whole egg was eaten up. When the third hare came home, his mother pulled at his whiskers, which were still covered with chocolate, and said, "You are also not the true Easter hare."

Now it was the fourth one's turn. The fourth one took the speckled egg. With this egg he ran through the wood and came to the stream. As he was running across the stream on a tree trunk, he stopped in the middle and looked into the stream as if in a mirror. As he stared at himself, the egg fell helter-skelter into the water. He was also not the true Easter hare.

Now it was the fifth one's turn. The fifth one took the yellow egg. He ran through the wood, and before he came to the stream, he met the fox, who said, "Oh, come home with me into my cave and show the lovely egg to my children." The little fox children began to play with the egg, when it hit a stone and was broken. The hare ran quickly to his house, with his ears hanging down. He was also not the true Easter hare.

Now it was the sixth one's turn. The sixth one took the red egg. With the red egg he ran through the woods. Along the way he met another hare. Then he laid his egg on the path and began to wrestle with the other hare. They just went plip-plop with their paws. Finally the other hare ran away. When the sixth one searched for his egg, he found it broken into tiny bits. He was also not the true Easter hare.

Now it was the turn of the seventh one, the youngest and smallest hare. He took the blue egg. With it, he ran through the woods. Along the way he met another hare. He ran past him and went on. Then came the fox. Our hare made a few long leaps and went further. He came to the stream. With a couple of hops, he jumped across the tree trunk. The squirrel came, but he kept running and came to the meadow. When the magpie shouted, he just called, "I must keep going, I must keep going!" Finally he came to the garden of the house. The gate was closed. He made a great leap, not too big and not too small, and laid the egg in a nest which the children had made for it. He was the true Easter hare.

The Easter Rabbit

Editor's note: Many years ago a parent shared this story from an old children's book, probably from the 1930s. Unfortunately I do not know the name or author of the book.

Once many years ago Winter stayed a long, long time. The children liked Winter. They liked to play in the snow and slide on the ice. But they did want to see Spring again.

"Let us go to the woods," they said, "perhaps Spring is there."

So they ran off to the woods, but they did not find Spring. It was cold in the woods and the trees were bare. They could not see any birds or flowers. North Wind and Jack Frost were still playing about. They tossed the children's hair and nipped their noses.

"Spring has not come yet," said the children sadly and went back to their homes.

A few days later they tried again, but North Wind and Jack Frost ran to meet them. They could not find Spring and again they went home sadly.

For a little while the children kept going to the woods every few days, but still they did not find Spring.

"Spring cannot be coming this year," said the children sadly. "We shall not go to the woods again. What is the use?"

So they stayed home.

But Spring did come at last. North Wind and Jack Frost hurried away the minute they saw her.

The tree buds began to grow bigger and bigger and burst into pale green leaves. The little flowers lifted their heads out of the earth. The birds began to twitter and fly about with bits of straw for their nests.

"But where are the children?" asked Spring. "Every year they come to play with you birds and flowers and wood folk. I miss them."

"We miss them, too," twittered the birds. "They always liked to listen to our songs."

"We miss them, too," said the flowers. "They love our sweet-smelling blossoms. They are good children and they never tear our roots."

The little baby rabbits said, "We want to see the children. We want to hide in our holes and watch them play."

"I know what is the matter," said Spring. "They have not heard that we are here. Someone must go and tell them. Will you go, Robin?"

"I would like to go very much," said the robin, "but I am very busy just now. I have to finish my nest. Perhaps the fox has time to go."

"I would go gladly," said the fox, "but the grown-up people do not like me. They would say I came to steal their chickens."

"You are right about that," said Spring. "Black Bear, won't you go?"

"I am very sorry," said Black Bear, "But the children are afraid of me. Besides, you know that I sleep all winter and have had nothing to eat. Now I am very thin and very hungry; I have to eat and eat all day long. But the rabbit would be a good one to send. Children always love rabbits."

"The very one," said Spring, "Will you go, Rabbit?"

The rabbit was just going to say no, because rabbits are very shy. But it made him very happy to hear that the children loved him.

"Yes," he began, "I will go." Then he thought of the dogs. Rabbits do not like dogs.

"The dogs will catch me," said the rabbit.

"Oh, no," said Spring. "You can go at night. The dogs will be sound asleep. They will not hear you."

"All right," said the rabbit, "but how shall I tell the children that you are here?"

Spring did not know. Then the birds and the flowers and the baby animals began to whisper together. After awhile they thought of a way for the rabbit to tell the children.

They wove a strong basket from twigs and leaves. They pulled soft green grass and made a lining for it. Then each little bird brought an egg from her nest and put it in the basket. Some eggs were as blue as the sky. Some were brown as the earth. Some had little brown specks as if they had been sprinkled with cinnamon. Over the eggs they laid a cover of fresh spring flowers, pink and blue and white.

Rabbit lifted the basket on his back and the birds and the animals tied it on firmly.

"Good-bye, Rabbit," called all the wood folk.

Rabbit hopped off toward the town. The streets were very quiet. Everybody was asleep. He did not feel afraid at all.

Rabbit knew where all the children lived. First he hopped up to Betty's house. He made a little nest of green grass. He put a blue egg in it and some violets. He laid the little nest on the doorstep.

Then he hopped off to Teddy's house. He made another nest of soft green grass. He put a brown egg in this and some wildflowers. Then he laid it on the doorstep and hopped off to Polly's house.

He made a little nest of soft green grass for her and for every other child in the town. In each one he put an egg and some spring flowers. He had enough eggs and flowers for all the children. When his basket was empty, he hopped away to the woods.

Next morning Betty ran to the door to see if the sun was shining. There on the doorstep she saw the little green nest.

"Oh, how pretty!" she cried.

Teddy ran to his door and found his little green nest too. And so did all the children.

"Spring has come, Spring has come," they called to one another. "See, here are the rabbit's footprints. The good rabbit came to tell us that Spring is here."

And they ran off to the woods as fast as they could go. They listened to the songs of the birds and they smelled the spring flowers. The baby rabbits and foxes peeped out from their holes and watched the happy children.

The rabbit was very glad that he had gone to tell the children that Spring had come. He has been coming ever since at Easter time with nests of eggs and flowers. That is why he is called the Easter Rabbit.

Nancy Foster

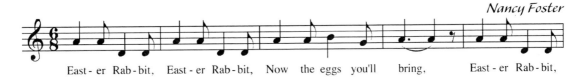

East-er Rab-bit, East-er Rab-bit, Now the eggs you'll bring, East-er Rab-bit,

East - er Rab - bit, Tell us of La - dy Spring._____

Bringing Easter into the Nursery: A Universal Celebration of Spring

Carol Grieder-Brandenberger

Editor's note: *This is an excerpt from Carol's 2008 master's project for the Sunbridge Part-time Early Childhood Training. It illustrates a nursery teacher's search for the underlying meaning of the Easter/ Spring festival and how it can be brought to life for young children in a developmentally appropriate way.*

Introduction

*I*n the beginning of the school year, when I met with a prospective parent, she expressed a concern about the celebration of Christian festivals in Waldorf Schools. This family was afraid that in a Waldorf school, the children would be indoctrinated with religion. It was important for me to explain in depth how we would be celebrating the festivals of the year. In our celebrations, I believe we need to be aware of how to observe the festivals in a universal way which does not conflict with the families' religions.

In *Living a Spiritual Year*, Adrian Anderson describes the concept of seasonal festivals as distinguished from Christian festivals, and points out that while some people are attracted more towards the ecclesiastical Christian rituals, others may primarily be drawn to the cycle of the year and the old nature festivals. He suggests that anthroposophy offers a deeper perspective on both Christianity and the seasons, and that through this understanding the contrasting attitudes might be reconciled.

It is helpful for Waldorf early childhood teachers to understand that traditional religious festivals have universal meanings and universal roots. Through the study of the history of the individual festivals, it is possible to find those roots and build a bridge between the cycle of the year and the spiritual and religious content of the festivals. If we can go back to those roots and meanings and carry them within ourselves, we can be true to the children, and not bring into the classroom symbols which have religious and not universal meanings and relationships.

For example, when decorating eggs for the Easter festival, it is not necessary to call them Easter eggs. Throughout different cultures eggs have a longstanding symbolism of fertility, which is associated with spring. We can celebrate the decoration of the eggs without ever mentioning Easter; we can plant grass seed without any explanations, and let the children be nourished by these artistic expressions without making any references to a religion or a set of beliefs. So as we celebrate each festival of the year, we can keep the question in mind: What are the universal truths of each festival which meet the needs of the children and adults of our world?

The Easter Festival

Here is a bunny with ears so funny
And here is a hole in the ground.
When a noise he hears, he pricks up his ears
And hops in the hole with a bound.

Easter is one of the most important Christian festivals as it celebrates the miracle of a divine being overcoming death. On a deeper level, Easter involves two great themes of life: the sacrifice of spirit incarnating into matter, and the triumph of the spirit over the influence of matter. According to the New Testament, on Good Friday Christ was sacrificed, and on Easter resurrected. Easter is a movable festival, unlike Christmas, which is on a fixed date; it takes place on the Sunday following the first full moon of spring, and is determined by a particular constellation of stars. (See Rudolf Steiner's lecture "Easter: The Festival of Warning" in *The Festivals and their Meaning*.)

The tradition of the Easter rabbit that brings eggs is one non-Christian spring festival custom which is still practiced within the context of Easter. According to Anderson, this custom originally involved the hare, a symbol of fertility. The hare is an independent and somewhat homeless animal, one that lives from plants alone, and never seeks conflict with other animals. The eggs symbolize renewal of life, and the egg shape can represent both the form of the earth and the solar system. Also, the image of resurrection is symbolized in the egg, with new life breaking through a shell. In *Festivals with Children*, Brigitte Barz points out that eggs had meaning in Persian, Egyptian, Greek, and Indian cultures, and are now the Christian symbol for new life after death.

There are many ways to celebrate Easter in a way which meets the children in their present stage of development. Young children do not need to learn about the facts of Easter, but we can bring the essence of the festival through activities and experiences. Easter falls around the beginning of spring, and it signifies the rebirth of new life. The seed children have been sleeping, and now are awaking to the arriving spring. This in itself is a reason to celebrate. Barz reminds us that it is possible to choose from a wealth of traditions and symbols for celebrating Easter which have been handed down over centuries, and many of these are so meaningful that it is worthwhile to revive them or to adapt them for modern use. Among them are the Easter tree and the decorating of Easter eggs, which we, in the nursery, called our spring eggs.

Stories of overcoming challenges for the greater good of others are meaningful for this season. For is that not the essence of the life of Christ, overcoming the ultimate challenge—death? In nature, also, we can experience spring as a sign of having overcome the cold and sometimes harsh winter.

For the seasonal story, I told the story of "The Little Red Hen." This is a story which exists in many variations; I worked with the version (found in *Let Us Form a Ring*, edited by Nancy Foster) in which she saves her friends, the cat and the mouse, from the fox. And with the help of the little red hen, the cat and the mouse learn to work with their strength united for the good of the community. In the latter part of the story, the fox gets two bruises after he realizes that the dinner he brings home is not the three friends, but three great stones. Bumps and bruises are also part of life.

Other stories, depending on the qualities of the particular spring season, could be tales involving nature, such as "The Little Brown Bulb" by Suzanne Down (from her *Spring Tales*). Nature stories involving butterflies might also be meaningful for this transforming season, but I would look carefully at what is occurring in nature; only if nature has actually awakened to the extent of the bulbs beginning to sprout, the first flowers beginning to bloom, and butterflies hatching out would I choose such stories. This year, with Easter coming early, the earth was still mostly brown, and most creatures of the earth were still sleeping. The spring nature stories seemed still to be a thing for the future. In preparation for the festival, we formed small pots out of clay which, fired and glazed, were used to plant wheat grass. Together, we put earth into the pots, and placed the wheat berries over the earth. This was followed by watering the pots, and within a week, the grass had sprouted and had grown over an inch. Placed on our snack table, the pots were in our midst every day and even if we did not speak about the growing grass, the children saw it. As a surprise to take home on the day before Easter, I felted little white rabbits, one for each pot, created by using as a base little white balls which we wet-felted during free play with the children.

The room decoration for this season was changed by removing most of the snowflakes from the wreath and replacing them with some raindrops and some decorated eggs. The nature table had been a seasonal expression of snow and rocks, with our nursery gnome and a few rabbits sitting there, along with the treasures the children had brought in. Now I changed the nature table to represent the barren Earth, still with the same stones, and the gnome and animals sitting in their safe places. A vase of pussy willows was fitted behind the stones to look like a pussy willow tree, symbolizing the beginning signs of spring. Felted snowdrops might look lovely on the nature table during this early spring season. On our table, there was a pot with bulbs which sprouted, and day-by-day we could watch their progress as the stems began to grow. Simplicity and truthfulness to the season seem important to me. Blossoms can still wait until nature is stirring more, and it is fine to celebrate the season in harmony with how it looks outside: if it is still brown and dull, our decorations may reflect that—with love.

These activities filled the four weeks before Easter, and with the activities, even without words, the spirit of the season lived in the nursery. It was like weaving a golden thread, and every few days, another small part of the artistic expression unfolded, as a part of the whole. And this is in essence what the festival celebrations in early childhood are all about: we seek for what can live through the artistic and linguistic expressions, finding its way into the play of the children, who thus work through and transform all they have experienced.

჻

Carol Grieder-Brandenberger holds a Master's degree in Early Childhood Education from Sunbridge College. She taught Waldorf-inspired art classes and parent-child classes before coming to Green Meadow Waldorf School, where she has been a nursery teacher since 2006. Carol enjoys spending time in nature with her two daughters and creating dolls and puppets, and as the Grieder Family Players, she and her husband are known for their traditional Swiss Kasperli puppet shows. Carol is also a Women's Health Nurse Practitioner and pediatric nurse with a background in maternal-child home care.

Celebrating Spring in the Parent/Child Class

Nancy Foster

Author's note: *Here is an example of sharing with parents the significance of the Spring Festival they will experience in the parent/child class. Since the parents take part in all the preparations leading up to the festival, as well as the celebration itself, it seems important to give them an opportunity in advance to ponder the meaning of the activities and experience, if they choose to do so. The verse at the end is from the* Spring *volume of the* Wynstones Press *series.*

The existence of death and rebirth is a great mystery, whether we are speaking of the resurrection of a divine being, of the cycle of human life, or of the seasonal changes in the world of nature. The meaning of this mystery is not one that lies open before us, given to us as a gift of understanding. Rather, to penetrate its significance requires striving, a search. The traditional Easter egg hunt is an expression, in a playful form, of this search for the meaning of the mystery of new life emerging from its dark, hidden place.

As adults, we may pursue the meaning of the mystery in various ways—through study, meditative work, religious practice, or artistic creation. If we wish to bring this mystery into the experience of young children, however, we will want to consider all that we know of the nature of early childhood. We will also want to be aware of how this seasonal festival finds its place within the rhythm of the whole year.

At Acorn Hill, like other Waldorf schools, the observance of the seasons carries us through the cycle of the year. We are nourished by observing and participating in the passing of the seasons in the world of nature around us. If we adults are attentive, we also notice seasonal changes in our inner life. In autumn, as the days grow shorter and colder and midwinter approaches, we may notice a more inward focus. This is a time of year for reflection and study, if we are so inclined. Reading or telling stories around a warm fire seems just the right sort of activity. We may even feel sympathy with the animals who hibernate at this time of year!

As the days lengthen and brighten, our inner lives change direction as well. We may feel a new sense of lightness and buoyancy, even a release, a breathing out, of an inner energy that has been keeping us strong during the winter months. We are ready to greet the forces of new spring growth and we stretch upward to the sun. The warming soil and sprouting leaves and flowers bring us joy.

Our children experience these seasonal changes intensely, though less consciously. Many adults can remember that indescribable feeling of "spring fever" from our childhood, associated perhaps with the feeling of the first warm rays of spring sun, or with picking violets and spring beauties, or hearing the first frog-chorus of peepers in the swamp.

It is a gift to all of us, adults and children, to take time to celebrate our experience of the seasons and to be grateful for the gifts of earth and sun, of nature and spirit. In our parent/child class we choose simple images and experiences which bring alive the spirit of the passing seasons in a way that can be shared by all of us, regardless of our particular family or religious customs.

To celebrate spring, we will be planting grass gardens in class. Waiting for the seeds to sprout brings a wonderful sense of anticipation and gratitude for the miracle of growth. Our circle time and story will also bring images of new growth, the renewal of the forces of life. Since ancient times the egg has been a symbol of the arrival of spring, carrying new life hidden within. It is a wonderful bonus that the egg's smooth surface invites decoration!

We are planning to color eggs with onionskin dye this year, using the resist method to create a leaf or flower design on each egg. Onionskins are an easy source of natural dye, and the process is quite simple and satisfying. These eggs will be placed in our grass gardens on the day of our Spring Festival and will go home with you at the end of the day.

At our festival, we will recall the planting of our spring seeds:

Rain flow,
Wind blow,
Sun glow,
Help the earth our seed to grow!

—N. de Bruyne

❧

Nancy Foster was a longtime teacher at Acorn Hill Waldorf Kindergarten and Nursery in Silver Spring, MD, and continues to be active in WECAN and in teacher education. She is author of Let Us Form a Ring, Dancing as We Sing, *and* In a Nutshell.

Celebrating the Whitsun Festival

Marjorie Thatcher

Editor's note: *Here we learn how a teacher has created a picture for the children of the underlying significance she finds in the festival of Whitsun. She notes how the world of nature lends itself to this picture. The verse by Margret Meyerkort and the song by Peter Patterson are from the* Summer *volume of the* Wynstones *series.*

⤳

The Whitsun Festival is the culminating festival of the Easter season, observed fifty days after Easter Sunday. This festival celebrates the descent of the Holy Spirit upon the Apostles, who were together with Mary. The Holy Spirit is traditionally pictured in the form of a white dove, and according to the Biblical account, tongues of fire were seen above the heads of Mary and each Apostle. The Apostles were thereby united and inspired to go forth and speak of the Christ. All who listened were amazed to hear their words in their own language, whatever it might be.

In England Whitsun was known as White Sunday, a Holy Day, for which the people in the north of the country prepared by whitewashing their houses and dressing the children in white clothes. The children gathered white and gold flowers and made garlands.

I have always been amazed at the number of flowers, especially white flowers of the composite family (plants with many small blossoms on a single stem) that bloom just at this time of the year. It is as if nature speaks to this festival.

During the week leading up to Whitsun we made white birds of white wool or paper. These were tied to a small stick, one for each child and one to hang over the snack or nature table.

On the festival day, either a separate table or, in a group of younger children, the snack table, was prepared with a white cloth. At the center of the table, on a round tray, a large white candle was surrounded by twelve small white candles in a circle, all anchored firmly with beeswax. White flowers surrounded the candles. At the appointed time the central candle was lit and the children were led to their places. Each child then had a turn to light a smaller candle from the central one. An older child or an adult would help a younger child.

At the same time the following words were spoken:

Flaming light,
Shine so bright,
Flaming light,
Give your might,
Make us strong and make us bold,
Turn our word to living gold.

—Margret Meyerkort

When all the candles were alight, we would sing:

We then had our "white snack"— a round cake topped with whipped cream. The candles were blown out and removed afterwards when the children were outside.

The festival circle time included the traditional singing game "My Pigeon House" (which can be found in *Dancing as We Sing*, edited by Nancy Foster). If the group was young, we simplified the game by using only arm gestures. Favorite stories, depending on the nature and age of the children in a particular group, have included "Cinderella," "The Four Feathers," "The Twelve Brothers" (all from the Brothers Grimm) and "Cap O' Rushes" (an English fairy tale), and for the younger children "King Adder" (included in this volume).

At the end of the morning the children took their birds to fly home.

I would like to express my gratitude to Margret Meyerkort for her suggestions for celebrating this festival. I have noticed over many years how satisfying and fulfilling an experience it is for the children in my groups.

Marjorie Thatcher taught kindergarten, preschool, and parent/child classes at the Vancouver Waldorf School for twenty-nine years. She is a co-founder and co-director of the Waldorf Early Childhood Training offered by the West Coast Institute for Studies in Anthroposophy in British Columbia, in which she teaches classes on the festivals. She is very grateful for the rich experience of festivals in her childhood.

King Adder

Editor's note: This story was contributed by Marjorie Thatcher, who found it in a very old story book, the cover of which is missing. Thus we do not have any information to share as to the author or publisher. Marjorie tells us that in trying to understand the significance of the snake, she found helpful insights in a passage about the fairy tale "The White Snake" in Rudolf Meyer's book The Wisdom of Fairy Tales, *page 209.*

A long, long time ago a poor girl was servant to a farmer, who was very hard on her. At first cock-crow she had to jump out of bed, and go into the cowshed to milk the cows, and she worked hard early till late.

One morning, while she was milking the cows, she heard a small rustling sound in the straw on the floor, and looking down, she saw a snake with a golden crown on its head gliding between her feet. At first the girl was petrified with fear, but she saw the adder eyeing the bucket hopefully, so she plucked up her courage and dipped the bucket down to let it drink.

It must have been very thirsty, for there was only a dribble of milk left in the bottom of the bucket when it had finished drinking. The poor girl took the bucket to the farmer's wife in fear and trembling, expecting a severe scolding. But to her astonishment, so much milk flowed out of the bucket that three large bowls were filled instead of the usual one, and even the farmer's sour-faced wife smiled at her.

From that day onwards the adder came to her every morning and every evening to drink milk. Whenever it had drunk, it gave the girl such a look of trust and gratitude that she forgot all her troubles and was filled with joy.

Things continued in this way for a number of years, until the girl grew, and became the most beautiful girl in the whole village, so that all the young men were in love with her. She fell in love with a young farmer and promised to marry him.

At last came her wedding day. The dishes were steaming, the musicians were playing, and all the guests were making merry.

When the feast was at its height, an uncanny silence settled over the room, for the adder was seen gliding across the floor, straight for the bride and bridegroom. It slithered up the back of the bride's chair and on to her right shoulder, and shook the golden crown off its head onto the empty plate. Then it glided away and disappeared forever.

The bride took this glittering souvenir and put it in her purse. From that day forth her purse always had plenty of money in it, no matter how much she spent, so that she became the richest and most respected farmer's wife in the whole district.

෴

A Summer Festival
in the Parent/Child Class

Nancy Foster

Author's note: *In teaching parent/child classes, I discovered that one of the special joys and challenges of festival celebrations is the need to create a simple and meaningful observance for very young children, while being mindful of seeking the essential meaning of the festival. In addition, I felt it was important to address the adult need for a cognitive deepening of the festival experience. This seemed especially important since at Acorn Hill, which includes Christian, Jewish, Muslim, and other families, we observe the Christian seasonal festivals in a way which seeks to address the universal in the human being.*

For me, Whitsun had always been a somewhat elusive festival, even though our faculty studied one of Rudolf Steiner's Whitsun lectures each year in preparation for our own observance. Last year—my last before retiring—our faculty's study for Easter was "Spiritual Bells of Easter II," found in The Festivals and Their Meaning, *and this helped things fall into place for me, giving me the picture I needed for a meaningful Whitsun festival in our parent/child groups. At a parent evening we made felted wool balls of oranges and yellows, and during class attached streamers in those fiery colors. The actual festival took place at an outdoor circle time on the last day of school, as described in the following article. The Summer Circle is also included in this volume. The verse by Margret Meyerkort, which was also quoted in Marjorie Thatcher's article, is from the* Summer *volume of the Wynstones Press series.*

I offer this article, which was given out to parents the week before the festival, as one example of how the thoughts behind a festival celebration can be shared with parents in a way that encourages them to experience the festival at whatever level is most meaningful to them, while offering them the opportunity to look beyond the activity itself. It was previously published in Gateways, *Spring/Summer 2007.*

〜

A s our parent/child class comes to a close, we will celebrate a Summer Festival. Although it is really still late spring, we feel the growing strength of the sunlight drawing us outward. We know that at Midsummer—the summer solstice—we will experience the longest day of the year, when the sun is at its height. That is truly the time to "dance with the flowers" and "sing with the sun," as our song goes! Then, along with the world of nature, we will begin the journey toward late summer and autumn, bringing us full circle to the point at which our school year began.

Looking back, we can recall our observances of the role of light in the passing seasons. We honored the strength and light of courage on Michael's Day and were grateful for the gifts of the sun as we celebrated the harvest. As the autumn days grew shorter and the outer light decreased, we felt the need to kindle our own light within by creating lanterns to shelter one of the sun's last sparks. The lanterns' light led us through the darkness, toward the time of our Midwinter Garden. In this quiet and beautiful space, we experienced the turning point when our inner light could begin to shine, bringing warmth and light into the world. Soon after Midwinter the days began to lengthen noticeably, and in spite of the cold, we could look ahead to spring as the sun's path crept further above the horizon and the sap began to rise in the trees.

Children feel this stirring much sooner than adults, but as spring arrives we too can feel, if we are attuned to such things, a loosening of our invisible protective winter cloaks. We feel drawn outward to the light. It is as if we no longer need to protect the sun's spark in our lantern, but can release it to meet the sun's growing light and reunite with it. Our own light begins to stream outward, like a flower opening to the sun. The sun, in return, sends its warmth and light down to us, bringing us joyful and healing messages from the heavenly worlds and inviting us to share this light through our words and deeds.

When we throw aloft our fiery balls with their streamers of flame, we can enjoy the sight, and

the pleasure of catching them once again. This in itself can be a joyful experience for us, and for the watching children. But it can also take on a deeper meaning if we choose to imagine the balls' upward path as a picture of our inner light streaming outward, and their downward path as the gift of the sun's rays coming towards us.

It is interesting to consider that both the Christian and the Jewish faiths celebrate their festivals of Pentecost at this time of year (fifty days after Easter and after Passover, respectively). The Jewish Pentecost, more commonly known as Shavuot, commemorates the giving of the Ten Commandments to Moses on Mount Sinai. In the Book of Exodus, we read of that event that

"Mount Sinai was wrapped in smoke, because the Lord descended upon it in fire." At the Christian Pentecost (often called Whitsun after the old tradition of wearing white on that Sunday) the disciples were together when, as we are told in the Book of Acts, "there appeared to them tongues as of fire, distributed and resting on each one of them. And they were all filled with the Holy Spirit…"

Whether or not we observe either of these festivals ourselves, we may appreciate that the image of the flaming light of spirit belongs to human experience at this season. And so, we join in our Summer Festival and say together:

Flaming light,
Shine so bright,
Flaming light,
Give your might,
Make us strong and make us bold,
Turn our word to living gold.

—Margret Meyerkort

༄

Nancy Foster was a longtime teacher at Acorn Hill Waldorf Kindergarten and Nursery in Silver Spring, MD, and continues to be active in WECAN and in teacher education. She is author of Let Us Form a Ring, Dancing as We Sing, *and* In a Nutshell.

Summer Circle
for a Parent/Child Class

Nancy Foster

Author's note: *This is a short circle for an outdoor Summer Festival with young children and parents, using the felted balls referred to in the previous article. The "King Sun" song was inspired by words and melodies in the Wynstones* Summer *volume and Elisabeth Lebret's* Pentatonic Songs. *The opening stanza is from A.A. Milne's poem "Happiness," and Margret Meyerkort's verse "Flaming light" from the* Summer *volume is used once again here.*

As early childhood teachers know, the words and music of circles (rhythmic games) are like silk marionettes lying in a storage box. They appear inert, lifeless; we must awaken them to life through the movement and gesture we create for them. It is best when a teacher or caregiver develops meaningful gestures for a circle to meet the ages and needs of a particular group of children, bearing in mind the importance of simplicity and the essential flow of one gesture into another. It would be difficult to do justice to these considerations in attempting to describe possible gestures, so we offer here just the words and music, ready to be brought to life.

In a parent/child group, it is usually expected that the parents imitate the teacher's gestures. The children sometimes simply watch, imitating inwardly, and may not be able to imitate consistently in an outwardly visible way.

John had great big waterproof boots on,
John had a great big waterproof hat;
John had a great big waterproof macintosh—
And that, said John, is that!

But now the rain is over,
The sky is bright and blue;
To the meadow we will go
And see what we can see.

Erwin

Folk melody

Tir-ra-lir-ra-lir - ra   in   the spring,   O - ri - oles-and rob - ins   sweet-ly sing,

Through the leaf - y bran - ches   you can hear,   Ti-ra-lir-ra lir - ra   ring - ing clear.

A little bird sat up on a bough
And said, "I'm very happy now;
"The sun is shining in the sky,
"And here is my nest in the tree-top high."

Nancy Foster

King   Sun is climb - ing high - er In - to   the bright blue   sky;___ He

mounts his splen - did sum - mer throne All   made of gold - en   fire,___ All   made of gold - en

fire. ___

(At the Festival, the felted "fire balls" are passed out at this point, and as the verse is spoken the parents throw them into the air rhythmically and catch them as the children watch. On other days, the verse is simply spoken with gesture.)

Flaming light,
Shine so bright,
Flaming light,
Give your might,
Make us strong and make us bold,
Turn our word to living gold.

—Margret Meyerkort

༄

Nancy Foster was a longtime teacher at Acorn Hill Waldorf Kindergarten and Nursery in Silver Spring, MD, and continues to be active in WECAN and in teacher education. She is author of Let Us Form a Ring, Dancing as We Sing, *and* In a Nutshell.

References and Recommended Resources

Out-of-print books might be available to borrow by mail from the Rudolf Steiner Library in Ghent, NY.

The Cycle of the Year

Anderson, Adrian. *Living a Spiritual Year* (Anthroposophic Press, 1993).

Capel, Evelyn F. *Celebrating Festivals Around the World* (Temple Lodge Press, 1991).

-----------. *The Christian Year* (Floris Books, 1967).

Davy, John. "Why Festivals" in Gudrun Davy and Bons Voors, eds. *Lifeways* (Hawthorn Press, 1983).

Prokofieff, Sergei. *The Cycle of the Year as a Path of Initiation* (Temple Lodge, 1995).

Sloan, Douglas, Betty Staley, Roberto Trostli. *And Who Shall Teach the Teachers?* (collected essays from a colloquium on the Christ Impulse in Waldorf education; Pedagogical Section Council of North America, 2007).

Spock, Marjorie. *Fairy Worlds and Workers* (SteinerBooks, no date).

Steiner, Rudolf. *Calendar of the Soul* (various translations available).

----------. *The Cycle of the Year as Breathing Process of the Earth* (Anthroposophic Press, 1984).

----------. *The Festivals and Their Meaning* (Rudolf Steiner Press, 1986).

----------. *The Four Seasons and the Archangels* (Rudolf Steiner Press, 1996).

Von Kügelgen, Helmut, ed. "The Little Series," compiled from the work of Rudolf Steiner, English editions published by WECAN. See especially:

Michaelmas (2004)

Saint Martin: Between Michaelmas and the Holy Nights (2009)

Christmas (2005)

Easter (2008)

Seeking the Spirit: Whitsun Inspiration for Individuals and Communities (2010)

Working with Young Children

Barz, Brigitte. *Festivals with Children* (Floris Books, 1987).

Berger, Thomas. *The Christmas Craft Book* (Floris Books, 1990).

Carey, Diana and Judy Large. *Festivals, Families and Food* (Hawthorn Press, 1982).

Down, Suzanne. *Autumn Tales* and *Spring Tales* (Juniper Tree School of Puppetry, no date).

Druitt, Ann, Christine Fynes-Clinton, Marije Rowling. *All Year Round* (Hawthorn Press, 1995).

Ellersiek, Wilma. *Gesture Games for Spring and Summer* (WECAN, 2005).

----------. *Gesture Games for Autumn and Winter* (WECAN, 2007).

Foster, Nancy, ed. *Dancing as We Sing* (seasonal circle plays; Acorn Hill Waldorf Kindergarten and Nursery, 1999).

----------. *Let Us Form a Ring* (seasonal songs, verses, and stories; Acorn Hill Waldorf Kindergarten and Nursery, 1989).

Gmeyner, Elisabeth and Joyce Russell. *The Key of the Kingdom: A Book of Stories and Poems for Children* (Bell Pond Books, 2004).

Heckmann, Helle. *Nøkken: A Garden for Children* (Center for Anthroposophy and WECAN, undated).

Jaffke, Freya. *Advent for Children* (Floris Books, 1983).

----------. *Feste im Kindergaren und Elternhaus* (Verlag Freies Geistesleben, 1993).

Lenz, Friedel. *Celebrating the Festivals with Young Children* (Anthroposophic Press, 1986).

Lebret, Elisabeth. *Pentatonic Songs* (Waldorf School Association of Ontario, 1971).

Petrash, Carol. *Earthways: Simple Environmental Activities for Young Children* (Gryphon House, 1992)

The Wynstones series: *Autumn; Winter; Spring;* and *Summer* (Wynstones Press, third edition, 1999).

Other books referred to in the text

Meyer, Rudolf. *The Wisdom of Fairy Tales* (Floris Books, 1988).

Saint-Exupéry, Antoine de. *Wind, Sand and Stars* (Harcourt, 1967).

Steiner, Rudolf. *Education as a Social Problem* (Anthroposophic Press, 1969).

----------. *How to Know Higher Worlds* (Anthroposophic Press, 2002).

----------. *Man's Being, His Destiny, and World Evolution* (Anthroposophic Press, 1984).

----------. *The Mission of the Individual Folk-Souls* (Rudolf Steiner Press, 1970).

----------. *Truth-Wrought Words* (SteinerBooks, 1983).

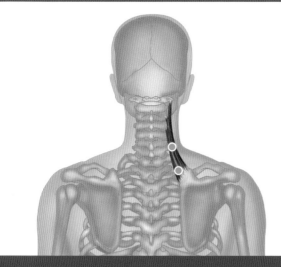

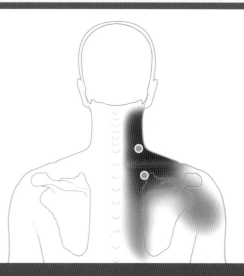

Pain Relief With
Trigger Point
Self-Help
Valerie DeLaune

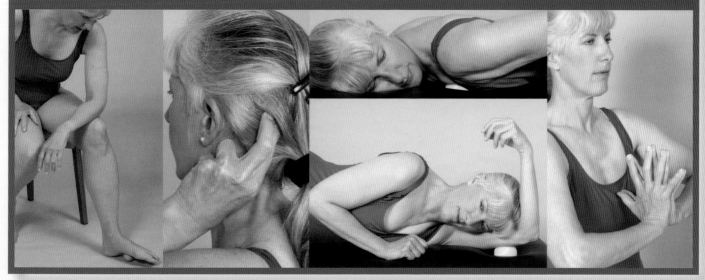